Contents

A BLUEPRINT FOR SURVIVAL

ESSENTIAL POETS SERIES 308

Canada Council
for the Arts

Conseil des Arts
du Canada

ONTARIO ARTS COUNCIL
CONSEIL DES ARTS DE L'ONTARIO
an Ontario government agency
un organisme du gouvernement de l'Ontario

Ontario

Guernica Editions Inc. acknowledges the support of the Canada Council for the Arts
and the Ontario Arts Council. The Ontario Arts Council is an agency of the Government of
Ontario.

We acknowledge the financial support of the
Government of Canada.

A Blueprint For Survival

Kim Trainor

**GUERNICA
EDITIONS**

TORONTO—CHICAGO—BUFFALO—LANCASTER (U.K.)
2024

Guernica Founder: Antonio D'Alfonso

Michael Mirolla, general editor
Anna van Valkenburg, editor
Cover design: Errol F. Richardson
Interior design: Jill Ronsley
Guernica Editions Inc.
1241 Marble Rock Rd., Gananoque, (ON), Canada K7G 2V4
2250 Military Road, Tonawanda, N.Y. 14150-6000 U.S.A.
www.guernicaeditions.com

Distributors:
University of Toronto Press Distribution (UTP)
5201 Dufferin Street, Toronto (ON), Canada M3H 5T8
Independent Publishers Group (IPG)
814 N Franklin Street, Chicago, IL 60610, U.S.A

First edition.
Printed in Canada.

Legal Deposit—First Quarter
Library of Congress Catalogue Card Number: 2023947532
Library and Archives Canada Cataloguing in Publication
Title: A blueprint for survival / Kim Trainor.
Names: Trainor, Kim, 1970- author.
Series: Essential poets ; 308.
Description: Series statement: Essential poets series ; 308 | Poems.
Identifiers: Canadiana 20230550320 | ISBN 9781771838627 (softcover)
Subjects: LCGFT: Poetry.
Classification: LCC PS8639.R355 B58 2024 | DDC C811/.6—dc23

For my dear friends A. and N.

I. Wildfire

Manna

I wake beside you. You ask if I'm hungry. *Tea? Cereal? Manna?* What?
Gathered like dew, like coriander seed—small as the hoarfrost on the ground.
Sweet like wafers made with honey. Shining like bdellium, *an hsi hsiang* along
the old silk road. You hold out to me a pearl of resin that will melt
in the sun, *unctuous when crumbled and bitter to the taste*, that will rot
and crawl with worms. But now, it is translucent and sweet. You
woke at dawn to find it for me, travelled through Exodus and Numbers,
Dioscorides and the lost botanies of Theophrastus. Hiked Bactria from Amu
Darya to the Hindu Kush, braved the cataracts of Nubia, the Erythraean Sea.
You hold it out to me—a teardrop. It cannot be saved for later.
It is for now, to eat in this morning light.

I wake beside you. You ask if I am hungry. *Yes,* I say. *Yes.*

North Road

We are on the North Road, trying to talk our way back to each other. I've
misunderstood something. You're hurt. I overreacted, I've hurt you. Sweet
dried grasses of Gabriola in high summer. Heat. Disconnected. Words. False
starts. Silence that is edged blue like kerosene, that burns with a clear flame.
I have not loved you well enough, your sweetness and your patience.
I make charcoal rubbings of your skinny hips, the hollow of your chest
and almond sockets of your eyes, these small imperfect offerings
of blackened paper. Later, you will tell me that I must understand
something about you—that you are broken, that you retreat into the trees
and mountains, into silence. It is so hard to begin. I don't know
how to move through this, but there is no other way, and we will burn.

Wildfire

The wildfires have been burning some weeks now, and even here at noon,
the light is sci-fi—burnt ochre, umber. The radio reports evacuations, but
none near you where you've been working long days in the west Kettle
and Similkameen while I have been carrying on without you.
You call each night from a payphone in the Kootenays. I cup your flickering
voice to my ear. Crickets, the zip of a tent, B minor sharps and blues, rasp
of white noise. You have become so thin. If I breathe too hard—
you are extinguished. Don't leave me. Come closer in tympanum,
love; come deeper, cochlear, sheltered in my hearing.

Wallflower

At the Wallflower, the night we first met, you told me about the void
and the shattering of the vessels. Gin bottles and fairy lights glimmered
over the bar. A silent black and white film projected onto the wall
mimed language, while our bodies began their mute communion
beneath our talk. Although I told you that I don't believe,
I have spent my life searching for the holy sparks.

Room B

For some time now, I have been trying to write a poem about Room B
at the hostel in Penticton where we stayed two nights when you did research
in the Kootenays, where I drank whiskey out of a green Coca Cola glass
in the shape of a tulip and we fucked and talked and wrote in notebooks and
fucked again and slept all night, our hips spooned and your taste in my
   mouth—
your lips, your tongue—my heart, after weeks apart.

But it is empty now—like words, like spaces between letters of the alphabet.

Little Mountain

In your version of God testing himself in the void, the scattered
parts sometimes join together—*fungus and algae sharing a skin,*
roots and mycelia intertwined below ground, lovers sharing a bed.
We spread a blanket in the shade of little mountain. Dried
leaves, prickles. Spiders pick their way across woven cotton.
Wildfire smoke has returned. The sky is pink ash.
A man called Isaac searches for holy sparks in the Galilee.
We lie together on this last day of summer and talk
alchemy, Genesis, the blue graves of Safed.
It is better that God is shattered. Glints. Dew in grass.

Ora

1.

The headline reads, **ISRAEL BREAKS GROUND ON FIRST NEW WEST BANK SETTLEMENT IN 20 YEARS.**
North of Ramallah, in the occupied territories—in Judea and Samaria, known as Amichai. *My people live.* But I hear *Yehuda.* I hear you read, *Come bride, hold something of clay in your hand for flesh dissolves and iron cannot keep.* The Hebrew carves new channels in me, guttural, plants seed. Your fingers spell my flesh. Your mouth opens mine. But will they know that *poppies after rain are also an archaeological find, rich evidence* in this broken ground?

2.

Descanso Bay. You teach me the blessing for strawberries.
Barukh atah Adonai Eloheinu Melekh ha'olam borei pri ha'adamah.
Say it again, until I can say it. Kiss me. Your blessing on my lips,
your breath on my tongue.

3.

You teach me the blessing for strawberries, fruits of the ground.
Barukh atah Adonai (Blessed are you Lord) *Eloheinu* (Our God.) Can you say it again? *Barukh atah Adonai Eloheinu Melekh ha'olam* (King of the World). I've forgotten already. *Barukh atah Adonai Eloheinu Melekh ha'olam borei* (who creates). Wait. *Barukh atah Adonai. Elohim.* Eloheinu. *Eloheinu. Melekh. Ha'olam*—I forget. *Borei pri ha'adamah* (who creates fruit of the ground). *Borei pri ha'adamah.* One more time? *Barukh atah Adonai Eloheinu Melekh ha'olam borei pri ha'adamah.*

Light in the tent flickering down.

4.

Feminine principle in Kabbalah describes a vessel that receives the outward
male light, then inwardly nurtures and gives birth to lower sefirot.
Kli—vessel—clay: build a tool of perception,
sculpt raw materials that can receive the light. This is
the necessary work. You draw a diagram: *hesed, gevurah, tif'eret.*
Draw lines: Kindness. Severity. Beauty. The light in the tent is blue,
is dusk. *The light adapts itself to express the particular nature of each vessel.*
Your fingers touch my spine. A ferry's wake hits the shore.
Open your mouth. Express me. I fill you. You fill me. Taste of salt.
Tif'eret. Yesod. Shekhinah. We are water and light. We are clay.

5.

You send me a photograph of the hills near Ora where you once lived, scarlet
poppies growing out of limestone like Tibetan prayer flags in the sere blue
of the Himalayas, where you trekked and studied Buddhist texts in silence.
White bloom of your shirt as you stand alone in the Judean desert
smiling at someone, not me.

You have lived an entire lifetime before we met.
I piece you together. The streets of Katamon as Shabbat drew near,
Jerusalem topaz and gold in the setting sun. Double bills
at Lev Smadar. Prayers in a tongue I have only begun to sound. How soft
the requisition green t-shirts you sleep in. Your rented room in Ora— אוֹרָה,
aleph, vav, reish, hei—lights up at dusk, radiant.

There is no innocence.

The moshav founded on land that belonged to the Arab village of al-Jura,
destroyed in '48.

I write this on unceded ground.

We are so small,

walking through a great darkness. Cast like seeds that grow
where they are sown, grow towards the fissures of light.

Boreal

You are driving into the mountains, into sunlight, into a storm, out of
cellphone range. Or you have slept in, still at your Airbnb in Edmonton,
in the green-walled basement room you Skype through. *I'll strip for you*,
you said, and you did, tearing off your t-shirt, turquoise earbud dangling
from your shorn head. You swim towards me through rippling teal light.
*Human existence is so fragile a thing and exposed to such dangers that I
cannot love without trembling.* Your sharp-winged hips. Black curls. Scar
of your circumcision. You are reading articles on the drunken trees
of the boreal, spruce tilting as the permafrost melts. Collapse scars.
Serotinous cones that require fire, warming, drying, death, to be reborn.
White spruce and black. Tamarac. Balsam. *Taiga*, 'the untraversable forest.'
I take a picture of you locked in my screen, a grim headshot. Send it to you.
I look like a hostage being forced to denounce American imperialism.
I put my fingers to my lips and touch them to your lips. *I can almost feel that.*
You are here. You are not here. Your body has disappeared. The finger-tipped
bruise you left on my collarbone is gone. You are gone.

        I lie in my tent at Descanso Bay, pitch dark, and
feel a gash opening in me, my ribs torn out. I am reading about the rhythm of
attention, *Our 'on and off' reception of the world, dynamic between mark and
interval or positive and negative space is also fundamental to 'the creation of
signifying forms.'* Here. Not here. Your voice. Silence. A voice. Hush. In and
out of earshot. Eyesight. *Rests and silences in music and poetry, like negative
space in visual art, are form-giving.* The rhythm of your body is withdrawn.
I resound in your silence.

        Strip for me. I have not even begun to know your body.

Blackmud

Maybe it went like this: the confluence of the Whitemud
and the Blackmud, a blank spring light slicing open
the snow, everything bare and desolate and dormant, and you
and me both out of joint—quarrelling.
                                    Maybe you'd said
it would be an easy hike, but it was hard, as soon as we'd crossed
the turquoise metal bridge scrubbed raw by seasons of cold:
mud, then slush, wet snow, slick ice, mud.
Bright spots—splashes of chokecherry and scarlet threads
of dogwood. A tiny nest woven with shreds of paper birch bark.
In the last hour we made a steep descent down a pitched tongue
of ice, grasping at roots and slender trunks at the path's edge,
then scrambled up a lick of mud. Glimpse of an oxbow
on one side, the rushing creek below.
                                    And maybe it was ugly
and beautiful, and there was still Havdala and a hockey game
to go. At the end of the night of this very long day before my leaving,
I cry in the dark, thinking you're asleep. And maybe you turn to me and say,
you're exhausted, you need to sleep, I'll hold you.
And then you sing Kol Dodi—*I was asleep but my heart was awake.*
The voice of my beloved knocks, saying, open to me
my sister, my love, my dove, my undefiled.
My eyes filled with dew. I was drowned in sleep.

Whitemud

The ravine after snowfall. Blue shadows and sunlight. Sharp cold.
In Edmonton, it has been unnaturally warm all winter, you say, but I
arrived the day the polar vortex edged west. The patterns are shifting.
It's why you're here, tracking research on the vulnerability and resilience
of the boreal. It's why I'm here, to be with you. It's too cold to hike down
to the creek thickened with ice, or even ten minutes beyond the trailhead.
Just far enough to see what you brought me here to see: mountain ash
at the trail's edge, clutches of scarlet berries capped with snow,
which, from a distance, you said, as you ran these trails yesterday,
looked like Vancouver cherry trees in bloom. I will remember this.

And later, in the dark, how you translate one of the psalms of praise
of one who healeth the broken in heart, bindeth their wounds, tells
the stars' numbers and calls each one by name. Makes rain,
makes grass to grow over mountains. Feeds the young ravens.
Gives snow like wool, scatters hoarfrost like ashes, casts forth ice.
For who can withstand this cold? You turn to me. Your breath warms me.
Hallelujah. Hallelujah. The beginning as the ending, always the same.

YEG

I wake beside you in the dark of early morning, last stolen moment
before enduring the cold of minus 27 and the drive to Leduc through blank
tamped roads and unfurling snow. I'll write this in my notebook
at the terminal as I look out at planes shrouded in ice on the blue tarmac.
Quick, my love, come closer, closer. Your flesh, my flesh. Sweet darkness.

Tonquin

You are in the back country, high in the Tonquin Valley.
I am tamped in this quiet space. There can be no signals
once entered. You gave me a rough sketch of your route—
a hostel here, an alpine road, a trail, a hut, a time to call
if you don't return. It's OK. I know how to be alone,
absorb silence. There's a trick to it, like writing a poem—a descent
into self while letting go. And I have things to do.
I dig compost into the garden beds. I drink Wild Turkey.
I read late into the night, of the *mysterious global Hum*
that began in the 70s—low-pitched haunted reverberating drone
heard only by 4% of the population. Is it external
to the listener, or does it come from within?
I read that the Arctic is locked in for a 5 to 9°C increase
in temperature by 2080, *devastating the region*
and unleashing sea level rises worldwide.
I read that the earth is in bardo.

                       Listen. Hush of your skis
on white tracks, sough of trees, first crack of ice in spring melt,
creaks, retorts, bird tocks and hoots, your breath. Then startle
a white-tailed ptarmigan, its cryptic plumage, snow on snow.

Iridium

Camped out all day in the foyer of the Centre for Interdisciplinary Science
as snow falls. Blank softness. Diffuse light. Drifts of people meet for coffee,
then disperse. I'm reading papers on the shore ice melting at Port Hope,
on the tar sands and the toxicity of the Athabascan river—*a landscape
resembling a war zone marked with 200-foot-deep pits and thousands of acres
of destroyed boreal forests.* This sticky viscous bitumen. This most destructive
project. Sea ice declines. Inuit elders say, *Something has happened—
the earth has tilted on its axis. The sun sets in a different place. The stars
are not where they once were.*

A level below in the robotics lab,
small scrying machines click and shuttle across tables. Glass office cubes
stacked above are tattooed with opaque formulae. The articulated fossil
of a plesiosaur floats in wintry light. They found this one in Alberta's
prehistoric ocean bed. Others embedded in the cliffs of Lyme Regis, Vega,
Svalbard. All were extinguished in the Cretaceous-Paleogene event,
a thin silverish glitter threading the badlands.

I can't read anymore.
There is no clear way. I will venture out along white tracks. Mark ink
on green-ruled numbered pages. Lay down strips of black carbon. Scatter
signals of plutonium and nitrogen, Tupperware, chicken bones, lead.
Absorb radionuclides. Take shelter. Mourn. Make fire. Write poems.
Conserve. Despair. Decay.

You text me—*almost there, 5 minutes.*
I wait in this cavernous hall. Suddenly, here you are. You have run through
the quad to find me. We head out into snow and startle one of the jack rabbits
I've teased as figment of your imagination. It flops away, white on white.
A plesiosaur floats through gathering dusk.

16

River Road

Tonight, as I walked with friends along the raised paths of the dyke,
Tetrahedron, Golden Ears, Mount Baker edged indigo and rose past wintering
raspberry canes and pumpkin fields and a bonfire's sparks rising
to first stars—all this which will disappear when the seas begin to rise—
I thought of the *nigun ga'aguim* you sent me last night, your voice small
and scratchy like an old vinyl recording, *this quiet yearning*.

Say Nuth Khaw Yum

I heard the falls as we paddled north in shadow cast by the fjord's sheer
hills, or we might have missed it. Tabu to look at, but you were drawn
by sound and current to water coursing down the rock's dark face.
As you looked up, I looked down, and water bloomed with sea jellies,
a hundred tiny slips of moonlight sown in black water.
I have read that the blooms are becoming more frequent as earth's oceans
warm, clogging the filters of coal and nuclear power plants
that heat them. *Even so,* you said, *at least it is life of a kind.*
New species will replace old. We will have to accept many changes,
as ecological zones transform and shift northwards. Hard to say
how deep they went in sounding. We are a translucid and
voracious singing flesh.

          We camped at Berg's Landing, near Bishop Creek.
I lay in the grass and studied the starbursts of dark-green moss
interspersed with tiny purple orchids. I had no name for them,
or for the lichen sprayed high on the rock walls, or the pale
orange blossoms like Chinese lanterns strung along delicate stalks.
And I didn't see the petroglyphs the man on the Deep Cove bus
told us to look for, *carved by our people.* Two Tsleil-waututh men came in
on a fishing boat, maintaining the site, doing catch and release. You asked,
what have you found? Lots of jelly fish—the red ones sting. Sculpins.
Chum and pink at par. *But they're mostly still in the river at that stage?*
They said, here the water's calm enough.

          That afternoon I sheltered in our blue tent
writing, until I got distracted by thoughts of an equation for a tattoo,
something ecological—a beautiful and spare equilibrium,
like Dirac's equation or the first law of thermodynamics.

You suggested the Shannon diversity index, but there was no internet
to look it up. We ate nuts and mandarins for dinner, with tea brewed
from the creek, spiked with whiskey.

                                                    Thinking now of that day,
as we shelter in place and Sars-CoV-2 slips from bat reservoir
to pangolin to human, it seems a world away. They say it's given
some space to the wild, though. Coyotes and jackals in the streets.
And orcas in Indian Arm, for the first time in years.

Widgeon

I wake beside you. The birds woke me. Steady tap of a sapsucker,
the same one I'm sure who watched us stake the tent as he hitched
up and down neatly drilled hardwood. And another I don't know,
whose call I first mistook for rain trickling into slough.
And now I'm trying to recreate it in words, intermittently, as
I read Mutlu Kunuk Blasing on the lyric, *an I, an emotion, an ethos,*
a character, a rhythmic pulse, as you sleep. Liquid truckling stopped—
low left high trill. Its *connotational resonances, allusive networks,*
emotional associations, rhythmic memories. Songbirds have two
voice boxes. Elusive licks and trickles. A clot. Creek, creek. *This*
is what poetry does in the first place: it remembers what the human forgot.

Paper Birch

These are notes for a poem I meant to write in August, but poetry
seemed very far away then. The BC wildfires smudged the shoreline
of the Saskatchewan—everything ash on the tongue, like cigarettes
or coffee dregs, and the sun a smoked pink disc.
I had not seen you for weeks except by Skype (*I'll strip for you,*
you said, and you did) but now in flesh meandering,
now talk, now silence, now climate change and
your research on the Boreal. Here's aspen, here's choke cherry, *Look—*
Is that paper birch? I asked, *No,* you said, then *yes, yes*
and here are my scribbled notes:
                         Betula papyrifera; small cuts
in the cream skin, like welts or gaping mouths
of blood, of rust; carved initials join lovers; a trunk stripped,
except for bandaged swathes over brown flesh; a square
excised, the single deep gash for leverage and a sheet torn off; shreds
of paper on the ground. *They were refugia,* you told me, *migrating north,*
following the retreating sheets of ice.
                         Tell me. Where do we go from here?
Score me with desire lines—write words for songs that have none
in the wrist's blue margins, sparse language of the tundra.
Sew me with tamarack and stretch me over cedar ribs
tipped leeward to split the river's tongue.
You say paper birch fires quickly and burns hot. Ignite me.

I think that might have been the day, the night you sang
for me the *Tzama Lecha Nafshi*—my soul thirsts for you, my flesh
longs for you, in a dry parched land.

Desolation

We are wandering into Dark Mountain territory, Desert territory—news
that a third of the Himalayan ice cap will melt no matter what we do.
The Greenland ice sheet is disappearing *at an astonishing rate*.
Only yesterday the headline read, PLUMMETING INSECT NUMBERS
'THREATEN COLLAPSE OF NATURE'—the insects might be gone
within a hundred years, earth's ecosystems will collapse.
Mauna Loa observatory measures 415.70 ppm of atmospheric CO2.
The sixth mass extinction has begun. Look—here is a photograph of scarce
copper butterflies. Here ice cleaves and slips into dark water. Make art
out of ruin. Retreat. Wicked problem. Look for mushrooms that grow
in the clearcuts and scorched hollows. Gather rainwater, raise goats,
eat beans. Die with grace.

I am reading little manifestos, anonymous pamphlets, stitched
booklets. One says, *there are feral possibilities in the cities*—cast seeds of
anarchy in the capitalist ruins, they'll grow *like weeds on disturbed ground*.
One says, we must head out into the wilderness, climb the dark mountain,
dig with our hands—*Ecocide demands a response...where are the poems that
have adjusted their scope to the scale of this challenge?* One says, *it is good
to die*. The wilderness can take care of itself. Consider the oriental hornet,
Vespa orientalis, which builds its cells out of mud and is most active
in the hottest hours of the day. Look at the bright yellow belt clasped
to its abdomen—the *obscure pigment Xanthopterin* draws sunlight out of air,
and generates a small voltage. One says, *In our hearts we all know the world
will not be saved*.

But I am not ready to die. I am not ready to concede
defeat. Rage against this. Raise goats. Pierce hearts. Make art. Plant seeds.
Green ruins. Write poems. Manifesto. Harvest sunlight. Be feral.
Lyric. Elemental. Wild.

This is what I know in my heart.
The night before we climbed Desolation, sparks flew up to the glint
of stars and I felt your song as current run through my bones.

Desolation: Two Drafts

1.

That night by Lightning Creek, at the base of Desolation,
before the ascent to Kerouac's *awful vaulty blue smokebody rock,*
through forest of western hemlock and fir, stepped meadows,
snowstorm and whiteout conditions to his boarded-up lookout
and the blank void, we lay in the tent hushed to blue, blueblack.

I was tired and hushed too, barely flesh aware of self but you
were wide-eyed, talking mind and the universe—how embodied
in every moss, lichen, worm, dust, star; consciousness
that could be measured, emanating from matter like energy. Locked
into a pattern released only at death, slowly—reabsorbed like human
elements, carbon selenium iron cobalt gone to ground, but even dust still
bearing the faintest pulse.
                          You say you don't remember this—only the fire
we built on the lakeshore, bourbon and stars, cracked
edge of the galaxy pressing down—but my sleepy flesh absorbed
your words. I said, *hold onto me,* and you sang *nigunim*
under the tent's blue skin and brightly scattered night.
And maybe we were angels for a time, winged and sere, sung
bodies under the awful vaulty blue. Scorched and desolate.

2.

Try again. I wrote down everything: ranger station at Marblemount
for the back country permit, salmon pink Bakelite phone fixed to a pole
to call someone over from the lodge to fetch us. The tin boat we motored
up Ross Lake in as the fall light bled out, and the mountains darkened
and tightened around us. You steered. I sat in the bow exhilarated, frozen,

keeping an eye out for snags. N. reclined in between drinking my bourbon,
hiking boots propped on his pack, talking political ecology and Marx.
At Lightning Creek, we dragged the boat onto the gravel shore, the dock
out of commission for the winter. You and N. pitched the tents.
I made a campfire of driftwood, pinecones, bark, as dusk came on—
a blueing light. More bourbon. Firelight. Crush of stars.
Back and forth from the fire to the dark beach to peer up at the drifting
galaxy. And then the part I've written about in another poem—
how we lay in the tent, hushed to blue, blueblack, and you talked
consciousness and the universe; except this time I remember you wondering
if when we die our souls, like energy released from matter, slip free
and join some larger force. Then you sang some songs without words
and the next thing I heard was N. making bird calls from his tent
to wake us before dawn, because we'd calculated we'd need every minute
of daylight to climb Desolation and still have time to return the boat
to the lodge. I wrote, *Cooked oatmeal + zen tea*. Struck camp. Stashed
our gear in the bear locker. The boat's motor wouldn't unlock. Then it did.
Navigating past Cat Island to the steep trail head.

And now the details are compressed.
I began on the lower slopes. Stripped off my jacket, hoody. You caught up.
N. trailed below. A clearing. Glimpse of Ross Lake. I was bleeding heavily
all day as we hiked up through switchbacks and dark fir. Sudden
patches of maple burning like embers. Stepped meadows. A tiny, fluorescent
green caterpillar. N. speculating on the IPCC's special report on 1.5 °,
on there being nowhere left to go where there is wild—untended, free. You
disagreed, kept an eye on me as it began to rain. Then snow. Driving snow
and nothing but the rhythm of the climb up and up until the trail plateaued and
we hit the shuttered fire lookout. Whiteout conditions. Hozomeen somewhere
in the void. I tried to take a photograph, but my phone shut down in the cold.
So I guess this will have to do. We turned around and began the climb down.

II. Seeds

serotiny: requiring the heat of a wildfire to open
—*Wiktionary*

4. FURTHER INFORMATION: Organizations wishing to join the Movement for Survival and all others seeking further information should write to the Acting Secretary, *The Movement for Survival*, c/o *The Ecologist*, Kew Green, Richmond, Surrey.
—*A Blueprint for Survival*, 1972

The blessing is in the seed.
—Muriel Rukeyser, *10th Elegy*

1. SHELTER

So I'm here again in the blue tent, the night before we climbed Desolation.
Jack's *awful vaulty blue smokebody rock*. Hozomeen looms somewhere
beyond us. The fire lookout boarded up for the season. Late October.
Angels in the bluedark. Glint of cracked mica slung skyward over Lightening
Creek. Something about this night I haven't figured out. Still the bittersweet
scent of woodsmoke, scorched driftwood. Fossilized sunlight and bourbon fire
on my tongue. Jagged pulsing spine of the galaxy beyond this nylon skin that
sheltered you through fieldwork in the Okanagan, while the wildfires burned
two summers ago now, and the summer after in Edmonton, while you worked
on vulnerability and climate change in the boreal—fire-quick, blueblack lungs,
forest *dominated by species (e.g.* Pinus banksiana *(jack pine) and* Picea
Mariana *(black spruce)) that bear serotinous cones and require lethal fire to
regenerate*…Skies clotted so thick with ash we abandoned plans to hike in the
Rockies. Serotiny. *An ecological adaptation…in which seed release occurs in
response to an environmental trigger*…fire, warming, drying, death. From the
French, *serotine*, that which comes late, that which happens in the evening.
Seraphim's continual burning. Bluedark angels in the tent's shadows.
I'm trying to remember what you said about consciousness as a form
of energy, a quality in all matter accruing or an embodied pattern held
for a time and then released like heat or light from charred remains.
You were on fire. I drifted. Qualia. Quantum entanglement. Sefirot.
Keter. Da'at. Tikkun. Glint. Spark. Sparks fly up. You're singing
a song without words. It runs electric through me out into the night,
out to the stars ringing like bells and the tongues of angels perched
on the shuttered lookout on Desolation.

                                        Is that how it was?
I keep trying. This is the fourth or fifth time. It comes alive
when I write it down—black cursive, scored. Patched with White Out.
Stitched closed, then ripped out again, in this notebook bought

in a dollar store in Penticton that year I first really began to notice
the wildfires. And then if I leave it and come back to it after days,
I see that it has died. Keep writing. It's spring now. The first of May.
Camp site 5 at Descanso. My bike and two ferries to get here—
Queen of Cowichen, the Quinsam. Salt. Tar. Dark-eyed juncos
flit by at dusk, a blurred flutter at the edge of sight. The tree frogs are singing.
Charred fire pit. Woodsmoke and weed. I've pitched my tent by a Douglas fir
and touched the furrowed bark. I come here to figure things out.
Y. called last night from Edmonton where he's packing up after a long winter.
We argued panpsychism, biocentrism, consciousness emanating from matter
or the world generated by our consciousness. *But then how to explain*
what happens when we go dark? When we sleep? Does the world cease
to exist? Time and space as tools of perception. Is this just Kant,
skewed by quantum mechanics? *How do we explain two individuals who*
seem to have the same perceptions of an external reality? He is a thin line
of sound that rings the small bones in my ear. Radio wave converts
to electrochemical signal. Wake of a ferry. Its throb. Wingblur
clips the tent's fly. Then something about the Lurianic hierarchy of souls.
Nefesh, the life force—the force that lingers at the grave. Immanent.
Embodied. Then *Ruach*—spirit, breath. All the way through *Yechidah*.
The solitary. A single point that joins human and divine. Transcendent.
And how we might catch glimpses of this, in prophecy or dream.
Is this another way to speak of energy? Y. insists on the existence
of an external world and objective, scientific precision. *Bracket the subjective*
emotional response. But I don't mean emotional, not like that. The subjective
cannot be bracketed. I mean attention as a moral act. To see
the radical alterity of things which are ultimately dark and withdrawn.
O blue clay of flesh. O dark-eyed junco.

I lie in my own tent, greeny chamber, like a silique
of the capsella. Shepherd's purse. Mother's heart. Weed
that blooms on disturbed ground. To be vigilant.
To know what it is possible to know of this other being
apart in its own being. O dark-eyed junco. O love.
The trees are singing. I hear. I'm listening.

2. CODEX

On 11 April 2019, the Israeli lunar lander Beresheet—*In the beginning,* named after the opening word of Genesis in the Hebrew bible—crash landed on the moon. Besides the DNA of a venture capitalist, and a handful of tardigrades in their dormant tun state, in which they are virtually indestructible, even in the void of space, the spacecraft carried within its shattered hull the Arch Lunar Library™, an archive of curated human knowledge, etched by lasers onto 25 stacked nickel discs—each one only 40 microns thick: 4 analog layers, the first page readable by the human eye, the next 3 with a microscope or handheld magnifying glass; the next 20 pages digital, the previous pages containing instructions on how to read them. The archive included the entire contents of the English *Wikipedia* and a wearable Rosetta disc, a primer to the world's languages. On the digital pages, each letter was said to be the size of a bacillus bacterium. Nickel engraved with optical nanolithography wouldn't oxidize, wouldn't degrade, was immune to microbes, chemical erosion, extreme cold. The library was meant to be a *backup for humanity,* and, if it survived the crash landing on the moon, might have a shelf life of 10,000 years or more; in the vacuum of space, of several billion.

James Lovelock suggested a simpler, autopoietic backup in *The Revenge of Gaia* (2006). He called for the creation of a simple book, a primer that survivors of an existential global event might use to rebuild a more, peaceful hopefully more sustainable, world. It would contain basic hard-won knowledge—of elements and microbes, of atoms and childbirth, of hygiene and crucial medicines, of how to collect and sow seeds. He suggested it should be printed on acid-free pages, in colour-fast ink, collected in a well-stitched codex and written in a language so beautiful that every home would have one on the shelf so that its ubiquity might guarantee its survival.

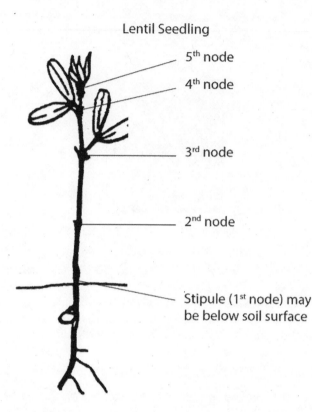

Lentil Seedling

5th node

4th node

3rd node

2nd node

Stipule (1st node) may
be below soil surface

The codex has served us well for almost 2000 years, from the Mayans and the Romans to the present day. It is compact and handheld, it lies flat when read, and can be printed on both sides, recto and verso. Its words can be read by the naked eye. It can be carried with you wherever you go. Codex, from the Latin *caudex,* means 'the trunk of a tree.' The Mayan codices were made from wild fig trees.

What follows is not a book of crucial knowledge, but it made use of the technology of the codex; it is a record of a stretch of days, from November 2019 through December 21st 2020, a document of global heating and the SARS-Cov2 pandemic, originally written by hand in a stitched, lined, dollar-store notebook

3. LENTIL

N. lives in the basement suite of a Vancouver Special, west of Renfrew,
east of Nanaimo. I'm biking up Renfrew after work on a wet March night,
bottle of cheap red in my pannier. N. has made a pot of dal and no-kneed
pumpernickel, just back from a Buddhist meditation retreat in the interior.
He has been hiking and tramping and trekking and writing on hydrodams and
Site C and commodity fetishism and keeping an eye on the carbon ppm in the
atmosphere creep up and up and up for years, for decades now. Outraged and
contrarian angry, funny, exuberant, dogmatic, accelerant. O my querulous
Marxist friend, what sorrows root, what rages, what ails you tonight?

(The earth is in bardo.)

Sit down at the kitchen table. Pour wine into jars. *What can I say, man?*
I've been thinking about this since the 80s. So we drink and talk,
talk radon, Shimano, Campagnolo. McKibben. Monbiot. Thunberg.
James Lovelock. (*He's a crackpot.*) No he's not. The IPCC Special Report on
on 1.5 degrees of warming. Fusion as magical thinking. Recipes for
pumpernickel. The war in the woods and Tzeporah Berman. *She was wrong*
on run-of-the-river. Meditation. *You just watch your breath. It takes years.*

---

purchased in Penticton in the wildfire season of 2016. These entries were written
concurrently with the writing of "Seeds."

Thursday 14 November 2019, 410.80 ppm
Thinking about the idea of the book, Lovelock, tardigrades, what survives, as my
students presented *Desert*—anarchist manifesto first circulated in 2011, predi-
cated on the assertion that "the world will not be saved." There will be no global
revolution, no green new deal, no system-wide change: "While NGOs are still
bubbling about stopping a two-degree warming, increasingly many climate sci-
entists are discussing a four-degree warming by end of the century, or even as

Sometimes I masturbate. The lovely Lily, Linda, Natasha, Chandra, Karen, Chavisa, Mig, Suzy, Helen, Stephanie, Jessica. *Oh, but she was so lovely….* Talk vegan diets and carbon gentrification, sequestration. The Pope's encyclical, *Laudate Si.* West Moberly and Saulteau nations. Endangered caribou in the Peace. *You just watch your breath.* The Bardol Thodol.

(The earth is in bardo.)

N. serves bowls of dal. Coarse sea salt. Chopped jalapeño.
Now we're onto the Green New Deal and Alexandria Ocasio-Cortez.
Is it a fatal error to link the dismantling of capitalism to carbon reduction?
The open letter to Extinction Rebellion, the Red New Deal.
I don't know. How can I put it? Everything's fractured, all these little splinter ideologies. The Transmountain Pipeline. Tsleil-waututh. Blockadia.
Naomi Klein blurs together all these different kinds of capitalism. Solar cells.
Wind turbines. Climate Leviathan. Climate Mao. Chlorella. Spirulina.
Trump is right, the cows will have to go. (Can we keep goats? I love goats.)
And we have to stop eating fish—the main protein source for coastal poor in the South. The Svalbard Seedbank. No-till farming. Bija mantras.
You just watch your breath. Thoughts will interfere and you just watch them too. The Greenland ice shelf. Methane deposits in permafrost.
Ecomodernists. Microplastics. Converting farmland to forests. Genetic modification of staple crops to fix more carbon in their roots.
My grandfather invented Krilium for Monsanto, he was the father of the Green Revolution! (The irony). The Tiny House Warriors

---

early as 2060." So it says, look instead for small spaces, opportunities, clearings, niches, where liberty and wilderness can be found; "there are feral possibilities in the cities as almost everywhere…the seeds of social movement Anarchism are largely carried around the planet on the coattails of capitalism and often grow best, like weeds, on disturbed ground." Later, N. sends me 2 articles by Bill Rees in *The Tyee*: "Memos from a Climate Realist." Rees argues that "to meet the Paris challenge of keeping the mean global temperature to less than 2 Celsius degrees means cutting CO2 emissions to almost half of 2010 levels, and doing so by 2030. It also means completely decarbonizing the economy by 2050." But the world economy is dependent on cheap fossil fuel energy and "neoliberal economics is ecologically blind." Green energy is not yet an adequate substitute. Result:

and Kanahus Manuel. John Bellamy Foster. Disciplining capital.
How good the dal. *If you don't have a pressure cooker, you have to soak
the lentils overnight.* The Zen Centre. The Salvation Army.
I put photos of my challah on Bumble. Calls for World War 2-style
mobilization. The Apollo foundation—more like the moon shot.
The Great Transition. (What form will it take?) Tropical diseases
creeping north. Sea levels are rising. Arctic melt. Albedo effect.
Existential threat. Climate denial. Climate despair. The dregs
of the wine.

(The earth is in bardo.)

Remember that time
we went to the Princeton? *Yes yes yes.* The Wisehall is busy. What's Up
Hotdog? too noisy. *Hey, the beer is pretty cheap at the Brighton.* Slip
through a cordon of smoke to sit at the bar. Talk methane and cows,
vegan proteins, recharging stations for electric cars, the Evergreen line,
global dimming, qualia bundling. *They called my grandfather 'Q', we had
t-shirts made up* (My grandma ran a boarding house in east Vancouver).
He was given a lab by UBC when he retired from McGill. (She only
took men—firefighters, policemen, loggers—they were her boys.)
Communal living, urban density, object-oriented ontology. *What's that?*
(An extension of Heidegger—) *No one believes in Heidegger anymore* (A
critique of Kantian emphasis on the subjective correlationalist and the need
to shift back towards the object, the thing in itself). *No one believes*

"the world can anticipate more and longer heat waves/droughts, desertification,
tropical deforestation, melting permafrost, methane releases, regional water
shortages, failing agriculture, regional famines, rising sea levels, the flooding (and
eventual loss) of many coastal communities, abandonment of over-heated cit-
ies, civil unrest, mass migration, collapsed economies and possible geopolitical
chaos." He ends by putting out a call for someone to prove him wrong.

Sunday 1 December 2019, 410.98 ppm
Stayed at Y.'s. Below 0 degrees. Frost in the morning. Walked into the bog. Pond
sheathed in cracked ice. Snowberries. Split rosehips veiled in ice crystals. As I
walked out alone, Y. continuing on his run, a dark-eyed junco in the undergrowth

in the thing in itself (Maybe that's the problem). *How can I put it, man?*
Kantian noumena is not the problem here (A way to recognize,
to acknowledge, the other. Heidegger's tool analysis—) *What can I say?*
We need to increase the carbon tax by several hundred dollars per tonne.
(Yes, of course but also—) Last call. Last call.

The first bardo is the bardo of life.
The second is an aspect of the first, the bardo of dreams.
The third is the bardo of meditation, actively pursued.
The fourth is of the moment of death.
The fifth, the *chönyi bardo*, is the *bardo of the luminosity*
of the true nature, a liminal state of terrifying vision
and sound, in which one seeks the clear light.
The sixth bardo is that of becoming, the *transmigrating form*
determined by the karmic seeds—bīja, बीज—*within the storehouse*
consciousness, seeds which determine the new form.

N. texts me. He's back from a radon conference in Saskatoon.
I'm at Descanso Bay, campsite 5. The dark-eyed juncos.

     Are you in Nanaimo? With Y.? Alone?

Gabriola. Alone. Y. is enroute from Edmonton.

---

at the forest's edge—soft breast, twig legs, claws, recently dead—overnight;
crystals of ice growing on head and wing.

Thursday night, 5 December 2019, 411.17 ppm
Reading more Bill Rees, "Ecological Economics for Humanity's Plague Phase:"
    Serious problems emerged only in the fossil fuel age. Coal, oil and natural gas
    have helped raise the human enterprise so far-from-equilibrium that (rising)
    demand for negentropy to maintain and grow the economy exceeds the pro-
    ductive and assimilative capacities of host ecosystems. The resultant entropic
    disordering of the ecosphere is evident in biodiversity loss, dissipation of soils

DAL SOUPS

Simple Mung *Dal* Soup
SADA MOONG DAL

This smooth, liquid mung *dal* soup is seasoned with a simple *chaunk*. It is easy to prepare and easy to digest, and its light consistency makes it appealing in any season. Serve it accompanied by a wheat bread or rice and a vegetable. To complete the meal, serve yogurt or green salad.

Preparation time (after assembling ingredients): 10 minutes
Cooking time: 1¼ hours or 25 minutes in a pressure cooker
Serves: 4 to 6

⅔ cup (145 g) split *moong dal*, without skins
6½ cups (1.5 liters) water (5½ cups/1.3 liters if pressure-cooked)
1 teaspoon (5 ml) turmeric
2 teaspoons (10 ml) ground coriander
1½ teaspoons (7 ml) scraped, finely shredded or minced fresh ginger root
1 teaspoon (5 ml) minced seeded hot green chili (or as desired)
1¼ teaspoons (6 ml) salt
2 tablespoons (30 ml) *ghee* or vegetable oil
1 teaspoon (5 ml) cumin seeds
2 tablespoons (30 ml) coarsely chopped fresh coriander or minced fresh parsley

1. Sort, wash and drain the split mung beans as explained on page 42.
2. Combine the mung beans, water, turmeric, coriander, ginger root and green chili in a heavy 3-quart/liter nonstick saucepan. Stirring occasionally, bring to a full boil over high heat. Reduce the heat to moderately low, cover with a tight-fitting lid and boil gently for 1 hour or until the *dal* is soft and fully cooked. For pressure cooking, combine the ingredients in a 6-quart/liter pressure cooker, cover and cook for 25 minutes under pressure. Remove from the heat and let the pressure drop by itself.
3. Off the heat, uncover, add the salt and beat with a wire whisk or rotary beater until the *dal* soup is creamy smooth.
4. Heat the *ghee* or oil in a small saucepan over moderate to moderately high heat. When it is hot, toss in the cumin seeds. Fry until the seeds turn brown. Pour into the *dal* soup, immediately cover and allow the seasonings to soak into the hot *dal* for 1–2 minutes. Add the minced herb, stir and serve.

and material resources (including fossil fuels), accumulating GHGs/climate change, ocean dead zones, etc., all signature symptoms of overshoot and apparent gross human ecological dysfunction.

Or, more simply, "We're fucked." But F. said this in a brightly ironic tone, as if the words untethered from the dark weight of their meaning. Because it is inconceivable? Because he is 15? A sort of optimistic nihilism. Almost all of the CO2 in the atmosphere has been put there since I was born. Rees:

Even if the world were successfully to engineer an economically viable combination of fossil fuels and renewables sufficient to double energy production, we still have a problem. The use of so much energy to expand and raise the human

A. is maybe in Edmonton.

I'm working on a new long poem.
Your recipe for dal will figure somehow,
and A.'s snowdrops.

Yes, lentils. beyond beyond meat
lies 3 millennia of food wisdom..
blessed by krsna shiva and ram
i am boiling split mung beans as we
speak. gunna eat with millet

yes! each section will be about a seed...onebeing lentil
i hope you grant me blessing to include yr texts in my poem

yes. go ahead better wven tham being a poet
is being a poets muse.

lentil is not a seed by the way

---

enterprise even further-from-equilibrium, would guarantee both disastrous
climate change and accelerate the parasitic hollowing-out of the ecosphere.
Bottom line: human enterprise will almost certainly be forced to contract by
energy/food/etc. shortages or foundering life-support systems.
And N., as we shot emails back and forth this morning—rare metals mining,
Extinction Rebellion sabotaging electric scooters in Paris, gigafactories, BC
Hydro buying cheap coal-produced electricity from the Americans—sends me his
own assessment. Sometimes he's optimistic, sometimes not:
*I haven't quite been able to get my mind around the big issue. We
have oodles of renewable energy, enough to support high-energy in-
dustrial society. But are all these externalities (child labour and land*

4. SNOWDROP
(Galanthus nivalis)

A jar of snowdrops in water. Green stalks. Chalk bells.
Maybe there were seven or eight. Sparse. In glass. I don't remember.
I have already used metaphor. It is not possible to know a thing
as it is within itself. There are sensual qualities, tentative approaches.
For me, it is often through words. *Galanthus nivalis*, common snowdrop.
γάλα (*gala*), 'milk' + ἄνθος (*anthos*), 'flower.'
The scape bears at the top a pair of bract-like spathe valves usually fused
down one side and joined by a papery membrane, appearing monophyllous.
From between them emerges a solitary (rarely 2) pendulous, nodding,
bell-shaped white flower. Scrawny and drooping. Like a floppy-eared goat.
Or, floral formula *P3+3 A3+3 ^G(3) chromosome #$2n = 24$
I don't really remember. I wasn't paying attention. A. picked them
from her parents' garden, or maybe from the side of the road.
Theophrastus called it λευκόϊον, white violet.
Violette de la chandaleur. Fiore della purificazione.
Medical students use it as a blot mnemonic: SNoW DRoP SNW DRP
Southern. Northern. Western. DNA RNA Proteins.

---

occupation by solar farms, mining) so bad that we need to resort to a
much lower energy society and a de-growth path?
In Australia, it's summer—and drought. Over a hundred bushfires burning in New
South Wales. Fires merging north of Sydney and threatening its outskirts. A pho-
tograph of the opera house in the eerie sci-fi haze I recognize from the Okanagan
two summers ago, and a red moon at the Sydney airport.

Saturday morning, 7 December 2019, 411.31 ppm
Bluedark morning. Rain. *The Guardian*'s headline: AUSTRALIA FIRES: BLAZES 'TOO
BIG TO PUT OUT' AS 140 BUSHFIRES RAGE IN NSW AND QUEENSLAND.

Sunday afternoon, 15 December 2019, 411.76 ppm. Active Pass
Enroute to Tsawwassen. COP25 in Madrid just ended. "Jamie Henn, the strategy
director of the pressure group 350.org, said: 'The level of disconnect between
what this COP should have delivered and what it's on track to deliver is appalling,
and is a sign that the very foundations of the Paris agreement are being shaken
up. A handful of loud countries has hijacked the process and is keeping the rest
of the planet hostage.'" –*The Guardian*. Current commitments will lead to at least
3 degrees of warming.

The outer tepals are acute to more or less obtuse, spathulate or
oblanceolate to narrowly obovate or linear, shortly clawed,
and erect spreading. Milk flower. Viola alba. *Perce-neige.*
Plantae Angiosperms. Monocots. Asparagales. Amaryllidaceae.
Amaryllidoideae. Galanthus. G. nivalis.
Contains galantamine, an anticholinesterase which counteracts poisons
and prevents the breakdown of neurotransmitters. Used to treat HIV
and traumatic injuries to the nervous system. *Its root is black*
but its flower white as milk and the gods call it moly. Dangerous
for a mortal man to pluck from the soil, but not for deathless gods.
It must have been shortly after I visited her in her studio
and saw her drawings. It was a small offering.
We drank red wine with N. and the snowdrops paled
to white smudges. Y. was in Edmonton. The stalks were invisible.
Also *Schneeglöckchen.* Candlemas bells. White ladies.
The ovary ripens into a 3-celled capsule fruit…fleshy…spherical…
opening by 3 flaps with seeds that are light brown to white,
and oblong with a small appendage or tail (elaiosome).
In the 1950s, the common snowdrop opened at the end of February,
but since the 90s they have been opening in January.
Transgenic rice has been created with the snowdrop lectin GNA
to breed resistance to the brown planthopper.
Its seeds are preserved in Kew's Millennium Seed Bank in West Sussex.
It is on the IUCN Red List of Threatened Species.
The pale brown seeds are about 0.4cm long.
Tasty to ants, who help distribute them.

---

4 January 2020, 413.45 ppm
N. sent me a link to a *Vox* article at 12:40 last night—based on an animation from
Carbon Brief—to show that the 1.5 degree climate target is 'slipping out of reach.'
If we had begun to cut emissions twenty years ago … If we had begun the transi-
tion in 1988… Now it is far too late. Australia is burning. Thousands sheltering on
the beach at Mallacoota on New Year's Eve under a blood orange sky.

13 January 2020, -- ppm (instrument down). –4 °C
Monday morning on the Evergreen line. Snow overnight. Polar vortex has moved
south—a symptom of climate change. SkyTrain delays because the system wasn't

A. lives in a little houseboat along Canoe Passage, Westham Island,
a few kilometres from the berry farm run by my paternal grandmother's
brother's son, inherited from the Tambolins who came over from Italy
a century ago to settle in the Fraser delta. A. approaches things through line
and shadow, chroma and hue. She has given up oil painting,
because it offers only one formal view. *They make what they call 'moves.'*
Instead, she walks along the dyke every evening at sunset, taking note of tiny
differences. There is an owl. There are lists of wildflowers. A sleeping lady
in the blue mountains…*like vigilance, alertness and sustained attention
are the ground of our being in the world around us…*(N., cranky, shouts
down the phone, *I don't see the point! How can I put it, man? Why not do a
political ecology of the delta? Do research on the port expansion?* I say, that
is your way of seeing). For her latest project she has taped squares of white
paper in rows to the wall of her studio, one study each day, over days.
Each with a pencil drawing of a snowdrop: scape, slender
pedicel, spathe valves, shadowed, explicative, unguiculate, erect
spreading. Inner tepals, tapered, shaded. Papery membrane. Rustling
of days. *Without sustained attention, the world fragments.* Cataphylls. Bells.
*Without vigilance, we cannot become aware of anything we do not
already know.* On the farm they grow raspberries, blackberries,
tayberries, black currants, blueberries, pumpkins. I went with my sister
just two weeks ago and picked tayberries, which taste like earth, river water,
hay, ghost of blackberry. When you crouch down between the rows
of vines, there is protection from the wind. The tayberries are a brighter red
and hard, then ripen to a soft mauve bruise. There are not many left.

---

designed for snow or temperatures below freezing. Snow on the tracks read by sensors as intruders. Sliding doors jam in the cold. Transit workers using hockey sticks to pry them open. *The Guardian*'s headline: OCEAN TEMPERATURES HIT RECORD HIGH AS RATE OF HEATING ACCELERATES. I recall James Lovelock writing in one of his Gaia books that the most accurate indicator of global heating is the temperature of the ocean. "Hotter oceans lead to more severe storms and disrupt the water cycle, meaning more floods, droughts and wildfires, as well as an inexorable rise in sea level …" And later, "Australia bushfires are harbinger of planet's future, say scientists … Apocalyptic scenes give glimpse of what would be normal conditions in 3°C world."

They are hard to pick and stick to the vine. Only the ones about to rot slip off easily. I move slowly down the grassy rows. Slate grey sky. My fingertips stain black. Avoid the thorns. Tayberry. Tayberry. Tayberry. Papery wasp nest. Two wasps. A crow. Tayberry. Tayberry.

Thursday morning, 23 January 2020, 413.14 ppm. Pouring rain
Dinner with A. after work last night at the Black Lodge. She's working on a project to save birds. Sees the birds in their migration paths to the Reifle Bird sanctuary and the delta. Port expansion across the water when she walks along the dike, carbide lights flaring at dusk. Imagines this smaller and smaller patch of land mass that all the birds aim for from across the continent. The Doomsday clock has been moved to 100 seconds before midnight—closest it has ever been. Extinction Rebellion placed on the British terrorist watch list.

kim trainor <kim████████@gmail.com>

Fwd: James Nizam | Solo Exhibition | Gallery Jones

A██████████ s <a█████a@gmail.com>   24 April 2019 at 22:02
To: kim trainor <kim██████@gmail.com>

Hi Kim,

███████████you are thinking of my drawings, and the slow looking at certain species. ██████████████████████████ Survival seems a better course than grief. I lean toward the latter, damn.

I've been hanging out around K's little reflecting pond, counting my steps around it (usually 100 steps, or 50 x 2). And noting flowering plants there and thinking through the place with a little book of drawings of grasses and dandelions. April is figuring large as a falling in love place in time. Gibsons has a thing with Persephone, and it seems tricky to think of her or name her, but somehow connecting to the page as grass-growing place, (where the grass grows out of the page), I can locate her place above or below ground in the drawings. Well it's such a pleasure to think in this way, with the paper, drawings, and words.

I'd love to go to a burn site and look for Morel mushrooms -- they pop up after a burn.

Tomorrow we leave for Edmonton and I think you are back here! See you soon, I hope.

xo

Saturday morning, 8 February 2020, 414.52 ppm (recorded 7 Feb.).
Ruckle Campground, Saltspring. Woke up to ravens in the cedars—quork, quork. Tremendous gusts of wind. A text from N. with a link to an op ed by Canadian academics: **246** ACADEMICS CALL ON GOVERNMENT TO ACT NOW TO AVOID GLOBAL COLLAPSE. A joint action by lecturers and XR. Calling for divestment, full decarbonization for Canada by 2025, a just transition, a citizen assembly, mobilization of Canadian society akin to that of the Second World War. I signed the letter. 247. Climbed out of the tent and tried to boil tea in the wind.

5.

(TINY HOUSE, CARACOL)

We learned to advance while still hiding until January 1. This is when the seed grew, when we brought ourselves into the light. On January 1, 1994, we brought our dreams and hopes throughout Mexico and the world—and we will continue to care for this seed. This seed of ours we are giving for our children. We hope you all will struggle even though it is in a different form. The struggle [is] for everybody ...
> —testimony by Maribel, at the Third Encuentro of Zapatista Women and the Women of the World, La Garrucha, December 2007

The true revolutionary needs to be as patient as a snail.
> —Rebecca Solnit, "Revolution of the Snails: Encounters with the Zapatistas"

The snails creep at a pace of one millimetre per second across the earth's bright and shuttered surfaces, spikes, ditches, ravines, hollows.

Earth revolves around the sun, a minor star, spins on its axis.

---

10 February 2020, 415.67 ppm

Wet'suwet'en matriarchs arrested as RCMP enforce Coastal GasLink pipeline injunction:
Police made arrests Monday on the Morice River bridge, the sole entrance point to the Unist'ot'en land-based healing centre
—*thenarwhal.ca* Feb 10, 2020

The revolution has begun. All along the pipeline, the Tiny House
Warriors are placing tiny houses to defend unceded Secwepémc
Territory. *We are going big by going small.*

In Chiapas, the Zapatistas form their caracoles. *Their revolution spirals
outward and backward, away from some of the colossal mistakes of
capitalism's savage alienation, industrialism's regimentalism, toward old
ways and small things.*

The snail shell is the same shape as our cochlea—spiral cavity in a bony
labyrinth receiving sound as vibration, transferred to nerve impulse.

A logorhythmic spiral, κοχλίας *caracol,* its shape unaltered with each
successive curve. The approach of an insect to a light, a hawk to its
prey. The Milky Way—the arms of spiral galaxies. Our corneal nerves.

*The caracoles will be like doors to enter into the communities and for the
communities to come out; like windows to see us inside and also for us to see
outside; like loudspeakers in order to send far and wide our word and also
to hear the words from the one who is far away.*

The words are held in the names of each caracol—*Flourishing the
rebellious seed. Dignified spiral wearing the colors of humanity in memory
of the fallen ones. The heart of rebellious seeds collective, memory of
Comrade Galleano. Mother of the sea snails of our dreams.*

Members of the RCMP arrested seven individuals outside the Unist'ot'en heal-
ing centre on Monday—the fifth day of enforcing a court-ordered injunction
against members of the Wet'suwe'ten and their supporters blocking access
to work sites for the Coastal GasLink pipeline. The arrests were made at the
66-kilometre mark of the Morice River Forest Service Road at a bridge crossing
a river along the 670-kilometre pipeline's route. Around 80 individuals have been
arrested at Wet'suwet'en camps along the road and at solidarity actions taking
place across the country. Coastal GasLink was granted an injunction originally
in December 2018 and the court order was renewed December 2019. Although
the pipeline received approval from elected band members, hereditary chiefs of

The soft parts of the snail are made of 81% water, 11% protein, 4% ash and other minor organic components. It builds its shell from calcium and canchiolin, over a blanket of nacre, *a resilient composite material... known as mother of pearl.*

To build the tiny houses, *supporters can bring carpentry/construction tools of all kinds to Spartacus Books. Some basic tools you might consider donating include: hammer, tape measure, chalk line, and clamp, wood chisel, pry bar, saw horse, chainsaw, table saw, wrenches, screwdrivers, pliers, caprenter's pencil, utility knife, tin snips, nail puller/cat's paw.*

Tools to build small things, tiny houses, caracoles, to resist the geopolitics of plunder. *There are currently 77 military bases in Chiapas, most of them located in the autonomous regions controlled by the Zapatistas or in areas rich in natural resources: water, uranium, and the barite used for fracking and the drilling of oil wells.*

---

the Wet'suwet'en nation, representing five clans, have rejected the pipeline and asserted sovereignty over the nation's traditional territory.

Tuesday 18 February 2020, 413.62 ppm. Sunlight
Protests continuing against the Coastal GasLink pipeline in Wet'suwet'en traditional territory. Port of Vancouver (Hastings and Clark). Delta Port. I saw a protest at Renfrew along the tracks on Saturday. VIA rail passenger service and freight trains shut down—for a week now? Shortage of propane for rural communities. Backlog of freighters with perishables in the port—food, pharmaceuticals. Rogue street demos that shut down traffic at major intersections

The snails never stop building their shells. Umbilicus. Aperture. Suture. Whorl.

Ten tiny houses will be built and placed strategically along the 518km Trans Mountain pipeline route to assert Secwepemc Law and jurisdiction and block access to this pipeline ... We are going big by going small.

The smallest snail, *Angustopila dominikae*, could slip through the eye of a needle.

The small caracoles act as models for the world. *We hope you all will struggle even though it is in a different form.*

The Tiny House Warriors are building something beautiful that models hope, possibility and solutions to the world. We invite anyone and everyone to join us.

The snail is building its shell, *spira mirabilis*, miraculous spiral. A window, a door, an ear, a word, a world.

The small are making new worlds.

---

for several hours. On the steps of the BC Parliament. Trudeau reluctant to use force to carry out injunctions, after the dawn raid on Unist'ot'en by the RCMP with helicopters, drones, machine guns. But also, a lot of dissent within the Wet'suwet'en nation, aftermath of the Indian Act—elected band councils versus hereditary chiefs, not all chiefs in agreement, one stripped of her status for supporting the pipeline, workers who want work and improved living conditions and security for their families. It's complicated. But it is also insanity to continue to build fossil fuel infrastructure—Coastal GasLink, TMX, Teck. We're running out of time.

6. YELLOW GLACIER LILY
(Erythronium grandiflorum)

Grizzly bears cultivate yellow glacier lily meadows above the tree line. The bears dig up the nutritious bulbs for food. Soil in which the grizzly digs has higher levels of ammonium and nitrate nitrogen than surrounding meadow soil and glacier lilies establish and grow better, as well as produce more seeds ...

> —"Yellow Glacier-lily, Yellow Avalanche-lily, *Erythronium grandiflorum*"

I am walking the Heather trail from Kicking Horse camp through alpine
meadows towards First Brother, retracing the route Y. and I took yesterday—
Y. with his book of wildflowers, slow ambling sweet seduction
of taxonomy. Thistle and pussytoes. The western pasqueflower gone
to seed—this morning's drenched moptops, mountain avens.
He said, *as you climb higher in the alpine, you go back in time.*
I'm looking for the patch of yellow glacier lilies we found yesterday
while N. and his new girlfriend S. hiked on to Nicomen lake and back.
They're all somewhere far behind me now. Dark Sunday morning. Mist pours
down the meadows. Pack heavy on me. Wet and cold. Alone.
Yesterday we trailed in sunlight, slowly patched words to shapes and colours,

---

Sunday night, 22 February 2020, 414.20 ppm
FPSE ad hoc climate action committee meeting yesterday. Declaration of a Climate Emergency. Divestment. Ecopedagogies. Signing on to the UN Sustainable Development Goals, especially #13, "Act Now to Stop Global Warming." Sign the SDG Accord. Vett offsets. Link indigeneity and ecology, sustainability and social justice. Decolonize the colleges. Determine an accurate method to establish a baseline of institutional carbon emissions. Establish incremental goals to achieve zero net emissions. Incorporate the climate emergency into local emergency planning. Decrease FPSE's carbon footprint. Create climate emergency committees at every local. Transit passes for faculty. Make climate action the Next Big Thing. Rita Wong was there as President of local 22, Emily Carr, and calmly announced

sepal, stipule, umbel. Y.'s better at this than me. Little white flowers
like stars in grass? *Fescue sandwort, Arenaria capillaris.* I see.
I think I spotted one first, in a gully, then more all around, suddenly
everywhere these delicate pale-yellow blooms like fanged angel wings.
Erythronium grandiflorum. Glacier lily. Yellow avalanche lily. Dogtooth
fawn lily. Skʼémǝth. Sxʷixʷ. Hʷikʷi. Máxa. *Moist to mesic meadows,*
shrublands and forest openings; montane to alpine zones. The bulbs were
sweetest after long, slow cooking; the seedpods said to taste like string beans.
So I'm scouring the meadows for torn scraps of sunlit yellow. Looking
back for Y. and N. and S. who have disappeared.

Mist pours and darkens down the meadows. Little white stars.
Primordial blue-drenched eye of the world.

A raven calls, *quork, quork.* A dark-eyed junco.
I'm singing to the bears. 2000 metres above sea level. O!
here, and here—the glacier lilies, not densely packed
like the moptops higher up—sparse, edging
bare clods of soil, scattered around the gully's sunken
runnel. I'm damp and getting colder. (As we left Kicking Horse,
N. hectored, *where's your rain jacket? You've forgotten the 10 essentials!*
Always bring the 10 essentials!!) Ease off my pack. Drink hot tea.
I wanted Y. to be here but he isn't. There are white-petalled flowers
with yellow centres. Thick wine-red stems. *Caltha leptusepala*—
a sort of buttercup. Mountain marsh-marigold, elkslip. Still colder.

---

she'd been in jail for 22 days for protesting the TMX; she later apologized for
being distracted throughout the meeting, often on her laptop or phone—she said
she was a guardian of the Watch House on Burnaby Mountain and something was
happening with surveillance, something going down. Kathy, next to her, teaches
horticulture at Kwantlen Polytechnic; said she'd been at the Port blockade at
Hastings and Clark, helping to clean up after the protests ended and the blockade
went down so neighbours wouldn't complain. I am not doing enough.
    Took the Canada Line home. Bought a bottle of scotch. Wrote up an article
on the ad hoc committee for the Faculty newsletter. Drew up a motion for the next
union meeting to strike a climate action committee. Drank scotch.

Some kind of moss? Why are there no glacier lilies in the lower meadow,
only above? Did something happen? Y. said only that he would stop
to take off his sweater, and never caught up.

                                        Now I see them, far off,
single-file, N. is talking—always. *What if,* he gestures up the meadow
stitched with lilies and moptops, *what if I decided to stomp*
all over these wildflowers so I could climb to the top of this gully?
Y. takes the bait, argues, *You would create a path for others who*
would follow, off the main trail—there's no need. N., provocative, stomping
on theoretical flowers. *But there's my need man, to pick a wildflower!*
To bag that peak! And they are off, Y. outlining a hierarchy of needs,
a continuum of rights along a spectrum of levels of consciousness,
the ability to feel pleasure and pain, this continuum of rights intersecting
with a spectrum of need—the need for survival, food, pleasure,
to climb a mountain. A being lower on this continuum can fulfill
a higher level of need. *But I need that wildflower!* You can kill
for survival, but not for pleasure. S. puts down her pack.
Y. and I have argued this before. I am thinking of the lilies.
What of inherent worth and being, regardless of consciousness, a flat
ontology. We cannot know what purpose means, how lily
exists and intends in the world. The bear digs soil, extracts
this particular delicate bloom, this yellow. Lily sequesters nitrates
otherwise washed away by snow melt, grows richer corms.
They have moved on to the Musqueam development of Block F—

Tuesday 24 February 2020, 414.05 ppm. 8:34am
BLOCKADES SET UP IN EAST VANCOUVER AND MAPLE RIDGE IN RESPONSE TO
RAID ON TYENDINAGA MOHAWKS' CAMP
'The economy is not a person so it cannot be held hostage,'
Indigenous activist Herb Varley said, according to the Twitter feed [for
the Wet'suwet'en Solidarity, Coast Salish Territories]. 'Violence cannot
be wrought upon it. Quite the opposite it is indigenous peoples who
are experiencing violence.' — *The Georgia Straight*

Unceded land. Protests against development. N. shouts, *A bourgeois desire to set aside land around the university. The whole forest should be cut down! Build high density units for the workers!* I'm so cold. I stop listening, try to signal to Y.

 At last we go. Y. and I quarrel. Where were you? I was waiting so long. *I didn't think.* I'm so cold. *My sweater*—The lilies— *I'm sorry.* You said you wouldn't leave me alone.

9th August. Semaphore Lakes.

You are opaque to me as the lilies, as this moth
just landed on the page of my open notebook, soot-colored,
furred, white-slashed, its curled proboscis dipped in yellow pollen.
I sit at the base of Locomotive mountain, writing here,
while you climb the trail marked with small stone cairns,
driven by a need I can't understand and can't follow.
You are opaque to me as the lilies—even
in your tent last night, as you came into me, as I opened
to you, your cells in my blood, your flesh in my flesh.
There are misunderstandings. I hurt you, you hurt me.
We try in all the little ways, signs, touch, song, breath.
It is so hard. What is carried within the seed,
what stored in the bulb that waits in dark soil?

@solidaritycst Come join us at Hastings and Clark after your work day ends. We are blocking access to the Port of Vancouver in solidarity with land defenders in #Wetsuwetn and #Tyendinaga. We are demanding that the demands of the Wet'suwet'en hereditary chiefs are met. #WetsuwetnSolidarity

Sunday 8 March 2020 10 am ("data too variable")
Suddenly it is spring. Chickadees and Stellars jays in the early mornings. The alder are flowering. Shoots and buds. Violets. Chicory. Cherry blossom. But I don't think I hear as many songbirds as I used to in the 70s, in the house on east

Ancient, near-indestructible 'water bears' have crash landed on the moon

Microscopic tardigrades, Earth's most resilient species, were aboard privately funded Israeli spacecraft

CBC Radio · Posted: Aug 07, 2019 5:28 PM ET | Last Updated: August '

A 3D-rendered illustration of a tardigrade a.k.a. water bear a.k.a. moss piglet. (3Dstock/Shutterstock)

56th—waking up to a tremendous, prolonged dawn chorus. Intermittent now—a voice here and there. An interview on the CBC on green conflict minerals and the increasing urgency of switching over to renewable energy sources:

> About 50% of the world's cobalt comes from the Democratic Republic of Congo (DRC)…although cobalt is not a classic conflict mineral, it has still been linked to child labour. It has been linked to violence, extortion, corruption. In December 2019, International Rights Advocates launched a lawsuit on behalf of 14 Congolese families whose children were killed or injured while mining for cobalt. The defendants named in the suit include Apple, Microsoft, Dell, Tesla and Google's parent company, Alphabet.

7. TARDIGRADE

Analog 1

These instructions contain four analog entries comprised of this set of instructions; the first three verses of *Genesis*; a human child's line drawing of a stick figure; a primer to a fraction of the Earth's 7,111 languages. Followed by a brief statement on existential threats and archival cultures, which has been hand-written in a small notebook, then translated into binary code and printed by lasers. Followed by a haiku. This poem can be read by the naked eye.

Analog 2

בראשית ברא אלהים את השמים ואת הארץ:
והארץ היתה תהו ובהו וחשך על פני תהום ורוח אלהים מרחפת על פני המים:
ויאמר אלהים יהי אור ויהי אור:

I've tracked down the Sustainability Committee at the College and have joined, with a deadline to submit my feedback on a policy draft by third week. It was simpler to rewrite it, within the framework of the IPCC SR 1.5. Will put forward a motion tomorrow at the union EC meeting to strike a climate action committee. The College must do the same.

Wednesday 11 March 2020, 414.49 ppm
@Keeling_Curve History has shown that carbon dioxide levels typically resume their climb quickly as normal economic activity rebounds. If there is any benefit of the coronavirus event in terms of slowing the

Analog 3

Analog 4

benih imbewu mbegu mbewu mkpuru mbeu irugbin tohum
тұқым тукум toxum тухмй spéxwqel sēkla sjeme ceme
seme ceme семя semo семена *semente* seminko semeno
semente semente ck'mém'llts'e насеньне winih iri
種子 siki yp frø zaad pitit pitit ᐊᕐᕿ
noob mag fræ tov síol frö máahl ᓯᒃ had sied saad frø
fatu விதை buto imbewu насіння เมล็ดพันธุ์
gesaat żerriegħa 종자 hạt giống anwana'a
ziarno ᎭᏣ זרע uri hua 種 თესლი
graine siemen זרעים ᐯᑎᓂᐦ
σπόρους voa abuur llavor sìol വിത്ത് սերմ

---

pace of climate change, it could be in the changing of people's travel
and work habits in ways that lead to sustained reductions in fossil fuel
use. Only those kinds of long-term systemic reductions will change
the trajectory of #C02 levels in the atmosphere, Keeling said. #coro-
navirus #COVID19

Sunday 15 March 2020, 414.25 ppm
Cold. Bright. Spain locks down over Covid-19. Italy using triage to save some
patients over others because they have run out of supplies and equipment. UBC,
SFU, UVIC, all shut down + switching over to online delivery of classes. Social

ccɲ৸ ਘਿজ ঽ৩০৭ बीज ښزۃ ঠৈৎ
fare बीन hazia ണ৳ peo बियाणे sămânță बीज

Brief statement on Existential Threats and Archival Cultures, written in a small notebook and then translated into digital code and printed by lasers.

First, there were handprints outlined in reverse by mixing a paste of red ochre and spit then blowing this through a hollowed-out bone. Then, stitched leather pouches to hold seeds etc.; then, scrolls, pyramids, and codices. These have all lasted millennia and were analog before it was cool to be analog. Then, came microfiche on plastic sheets that will probably degrade or melt in about a hundred years or in the event of a catastrophic event. In the meantime, along came digital formats, 0s and 1s punched into IBM cards by female keypunchers like my mother circa 1974; then, microchips and thumb drives. Information coded in synthetic DNA or grafted onto the DNA of living plants, such as *Nicotiana benthamiana* (common tobacco) that can in theory grow whole libraries from seeds. (*Imagine walking through a park that is actually a library—every plant, flower and shrub full of archived information.*) Then back to analog again with optical nanolithography, letters the size of a bacillus bacterium etched onto

---

distancing. R-0. Flatten the curve. Bill McKibben was on the radio to talk about the one bright side—less carbon emission, fewer flights, less congestion on the roads. If only we could mobilize like this on a global scale to stop the planet's burning.

The Wilderness Committee sent me a packet of seeds as part of their bee campaign, *Native Seeds for Pollinators, Western Blend:* Rocky Mountain bee-plant, dwarf godetia, fleabane daisy, prairie coneflower, Lewis flax:

Native pollinators and plants evolved together but colonialism disrupted their relationships. With natural habitats gone, new species introduced and toxic pesticides, the impacts are drastic...Tricolour bumblebees fly as far as 20km to forage when food is scarce. Let's put in just as much work to help heal wild spaces—plant these seeds for the bees!

glass and then filigreed with atoms of nickel; layers and layers of this stuck together with epoxy resin holding the DNA and hair follicles of a venture capitalist, as well as a pinch of tardigrades who also, in their dormant state, have their cells replaced by a protein that resembles glass—and all of this shot to the moon on the Beresheet rocket, which crashed 11 April 2019. Probably the tardigrades survived.

Haiku for the Beresheet lander

Moon's lunar
Lunar of the bears!
the survive's carried through
        —*after Issa**

* www.languageisavirus.com/interactive-haiku-generator.php

Wednesday 18 March 2020, 414.60 ppm. 7:30am
More cold bright days. The streets empty. The US-Canadian border closed now, at last, and we are also in lockdown. International measures. Social distancing. Social isolation. Shelter in place. US army corps of engineers called out to create field hospitals. Naval hospitals called to position themselves on either side of the American continent, one off the New York coast. Triage in Italy. Lockdown in Spain, in France. Macron: *Nous sommes en guerre pas contre une autre nation, mais contre un ennemi invincible et insaisissable.*

Work at home. Stay home. Buy only what you need. Be kind. Trudeau comes out of quarantine every morning to announce new measures. Perfume factories and breweries making hand sanitizer. 3D printers printing hospital masks.

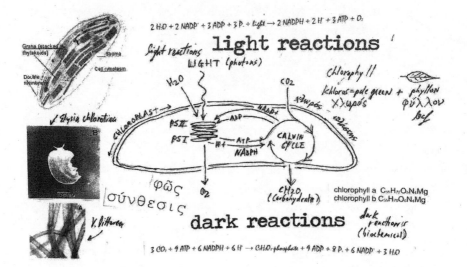

Hospitals bracing for a spike in COVID-19 patients, as the graphs and models predict. Yet nothing happens. Yet we're told it will come.

Thursday 19 March 2020, 413.75 ppm. 7:50am
N. sends me a link to an open forum on COVID-19: *Might there be emerging a window of opportunity to alter the trajectory of global development with respect to consumption and lifestyles, especially in relatively affluent countries?* N. says, we've always been thinking of a planned transition, not a spontaneous one. Maybe it will happen this way. Within a week, everything has changed. Stock market crashing. Price of oil crashing. Flights grounded. People aren't driving, aren't buying.

8. ELYSIA CHLOROTICA

(chloroplast, endosymbiont)

The light reactions, the dark reactions, leaf unfurling, the light—
eastern emerald Elysia, clade Sacoglossa, *Elysia chlorotica*
littoral, in the salt marshes, the tidal marshes, small pools and shallow creeks,
leaf unfurling, the light—the pigment chlorophyll absorbs the blues,
the reds, the spectral blues; absorbs a photon, lose electron flows
to pheophytin to a quinone, flow electrons flow the light reactions.
In the salt marshes of Texas among the blue crabs and the mud crabs.
In the tidal marshes of Nova Scotia. Vanishing. Cryptic green
algal endosymbiont. Seaweed. Sea green.
Chloroplasts sucked out and stitched to tubules like leaf veins.
Shifting genes. Diverticula. Radula. Algal plastids. The lumen,
the lumen. A leaf unfurling. Pale green χλωρός *khloros,* seagreen, moss
and pickle. Emerald. Pistachio and pesto. Chlorophyll. Love for this.
The light—absorb the blues, absorb a photon, lose electron flow

---

Teleconferencing. Zoom. Skype. Bluejeans. A message from the college to ask if we
are ready to teach the summer term online. New patterns emerging. Shelter in place.

Wednesday 25 March 2020, 415.22ppm. Morning
Sunlight. Chickadees—one high piercing note, one low. Dark pink buds of the
flowering quince.

Saturday 28 March 2020, 415.62ppm
> CORONAVIRUS: SPANISH AUTHORITIES HOPE CASES PEAKING,
> AS GLOBAL NUMBERS EXCEED 600,000 *(The Guardian)*

to phenophytin flow to quinone flow electrons, gathering. Illumined.
A drop of water split. Regain electron. A molecule, dioxygen.
The light reactions, the dark reactions, leaf unfurling, the dark—
realm of the dead, the fields of bliss, Elysium. The dark
reactions. Flow electrons, chain reactions, break down carbon.
Break down carbon, sweet conversion in the dark and
in the light. Endosymbiont who puts the light together.
χλωρός + πλάστης. Chloroplast. The one who forms.

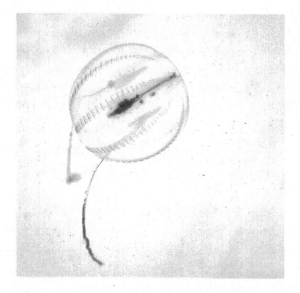

Reports that SARS-CoV-2 originated in a bat, transferred to a pangolin, sold in
a wet market in China. Zoonoses—human infections originating in animals—the
result of increasing human spread into marginalized wilderness zones.

Drove M. to her shift at the Wildlife Shelter at Deer Lake. A heron at the edge
of the road, still, hunting in the water-filled ditch.

Wednesday 1 April 2020, 415.77 ppm
CORONAVIRUS: GREATEST TEST SINCE WORLD WAR TWO, SAYS UN CHIEF
He underscored that developed countries must assist those less de-
veloped, or potentially 'face the nightmare of the disease spreading

9. THE BEAUTIFUL CELL
(I-glass)

9.1   *There is the same difference between a pain that someone tells me about and a pain that I feel as there is between the red that I see and the being red of this red leather box. Being red is for it what hurting is for me.*

9.2   The extremely tiny, mostly transparent sea angel, *clione limacina*, is actually a slug. It ranges in size from 1.2 to 3 cm and preys on sea butterflies. *Every angel is terrifying.*

9.3   *Just as there is an I-John Doe, there is also an I-red, an I-water, and an I-star. Everything, from a point of view within itself, is an 'I.'*

9.4   *Limacina helicina,* or sea butterfly—actually a snail—swims to a depth of 3,718 m. Its shells are dissolving due to ocean acidification.

9.5   The sea salp, *love child of slugs and jellyfish*—aka sea walnut, blob, jellyball, *goo of stealth, jelly bean of the sea*—forms eerie luminous chains and may play a significant role in carbon sequestration.

---

like wildfire in the global South with millions of deaths and the prospect of the disease re-emerging where it was previously suppressed.
—BBC

Thursday 2 April 2020, 415.41ppm
COVID-19 GLOBAL CASES: 1,013,157

Friday 3 April 2020, 415.02 ppm
I talk with my sister in the afternoon. She tells me Trump has ordered 3M to stop exporting N95 respirator masks to Canada and Latin America. That the CBC is

9.6   *The aesthetic object is inwardness as such—it is each thing as 'I.'"*

9.7   *Aurelia aurita*, moon jelly, is not a fish. It looks like the moon when light pours through.

9.8   A sea gooseberry drifts like the barred spiral galaxy NGC 1398, 65 million light years from Earth.

9.9   The glasswing butterfly is known in Spanish as *espejitos*, 'little mirrors.' A chaotic nanostructure makes its wings clearer than glass.

9.10   *The essence of glass lies in its serving as a passage to other objects: its nature is not to be itself but other things.*

9.11   Look through the transparent belly of a glass frog—little window into its body.

9.12   *This example of the glass can help us understand intellectually what, with perfect and simple evidence, is given us in art: an object with the double condition of being transparent and of having what is seen through it be itself, not something else.*

9.13   Glass octopus. Glass catfish—with a hand lens you can see its beating heart.

---

reporting there may be problems with supply chains, maybe food supply shortages. That the fastest selling items in the US are guns and ammunition. She's afraid that as COVID-19 slams through the US like a tidal wave, the Empire will implode. *And we're way too fucking close to them.* She's a catastrophist. But it seems not impossible.

Saturday 4 April 2020, 415.89 ppm
At Y.'s. Woke at 5—almost every day now, after waking every hour through the night. Dawn. Flat grey light. Chickadees. Last night we walked into the bog, following the call of the Pacific tree frogs. Y. has been hearing them for several weeks now. Little patches of song in the darkness. Went off trail through a stretch

9.14 *This object that can be seen through itself, this aesthetic object, is found in elementary form in metaphor...*

9.15 *... metaphor is the elementary aesthetic object, the beautiful cell ...*

9.16 I-sea angel, I-moon jelly, I-salp, I-frog, I-glass.

---

of blackberries the boggers are cutting down. Sneakers sinking into mud at the water's edge. They kept singing. Close enough to make out individual voices. Suddenly quenched—a long whispered pause. Then a single, high-pitched *creeeeek*. Another. More. More. Singing.

Tuesday 7 April 2020, 415.71 ppm
All the beets, radishes, basil, cheery and Roma tomatoes I planted as seeds last week have germinated. The sunflower seedlings are already an inch tall.

Almost two-thirds of the earth's population shelters in place.

Bodies piled in the streets of Guayaquil, Ecuador.

It's just a matter of time. If somebody gets it down here, it will spread like

10. SIIT, TUUXUPT, SITKA SPRUCE
(Picea sitchensis)

Even when philosophers turn their attention to understanding life processes, they largely ignore trees or relegate them to the periphery. In his *Critique of the Power of Judgment* (1790), Immanuel Kant regards trees as 'self-organising' but not as 'alive'—because they lack an essential characteristic of life: desire (which animals possess). In *The Phenomenon of Life* (1966), Hans Jonas argues that plants don't possess a 'world' because they can't be contrasted with their environments. Thus, while the animal-environment relation is one between a sensing, directed subject and a 'world', the plant-environment relation is between a nonsubject and nonobjects, or as Jonas puts it: 'consists of adjacent matter and impinging forces'.
>   —Dalia Nassar and Margaret M Barbour, "Rooted: The Embodied Knowledge of Trees" *Aeon* https://aeon.co/essays/what-can-an-embodied-history-of-trees-teach-us-about-life

Strange as it might sound at first hearing, there doesn't seem to be a candidate for being the intrinsic nature of matter other than consciousness…
>   —Philip Goff, *Galileo's Error: Foundations for a New Science of Consciousness*, 2019

---

wildfire because you are in lineups, you are passing by guys, guys are passing dope. It's going to be brutal down here.
—Kevin Doig, resident of the Downtown Eastside.
Cherry blossoms blooming over the tent city in Oppenheimer Park.

Saturday 11 April 2020, 416.09 ppm
A Hong Kong graffito:
>   There can be no return to normal because
>   normal was the problem in the first place.

I. *Juan de Fuca Trail*

The first time I really saw black bears up close was in the back country
along the Juan de Fuca trail, in the unceded land of the Pacheedaht—
Children of the Sea Foam. We arrived at West Sombrio in the dark
of shoulder season and pitched our tent in a high nook surrounded
by Sitka spruce, hemlock, suck and hush of the Pacific, woodsmoke
from surfers who tended their bonfire day and night and never
seemed to sleep. Bobbing up and down in the surf like strange seabirds
the next morning, all facing the shoreline in their black wetsuits when I woke
and looked out to sea, as if they'd been waiting for me.
There was only just enough room for the tent and a small clearing
to set down our packs and stake the fly. It had rained
through the night, but the trees sheltered us. Y. showed me how to tell
the tree from the bark—hemlock's thin grooves, not as deep or pronounced
as Douglas fir, although younger trees might look similar. Sitka spruce
like the scales of a fish—smoother, purplish-grey. Indigenous
to the coastal fog belt. I didn't know then its traditional uses—
its shallow roots plaited into watertight hats and baskets, ropes,
fishing lines, twine for sewing the baskets and boxes; its softened pitch
to caulk boats and harpoons and soothe burns; its wood carved
into canoes—just that it kept us dry all night. *Dark glaucous blue-green*
glint of magnesium drawn from the ectomycorrhizal threads of *Thelephora
terrestris* entwined in its shallow roots, as if when I pressed my ear
to the tent's floor that night I could hear the tamped crackling, or

---

Tuesday 14 April 2020, 416.02 ppm
I wake every morning at dawn and hear the birds. High sweet two-tones of the
chickadees. I text a link to N:
> HOW CORONAVIRUS ALMOST BROUGHT DOWN THE GLOBAL
> FINANICAL SYSTEM.
I only understand half of it, but say it seems to illustrate how the economy is
largely a fiction built on the illusion of growth. N. responds:
```
I read that this morning. it's an amazing story/article.
Keynes has some famous quotes about perception driving
capitalist growth. I am a realist about capitalism—growth
```

trace streaks of phosphorescence through the nylon with my fingertips. Y. cooked oatmeal. I made tea. Holed up in the tent with a book and papers until sunlight broke through at noon and we headed west from Sombrio towards Little Kurtshe. It was on the way back, just a hundred metres from camp, that I felt her presence as she flipped over clumps of seaweed and kelp bulbs at the hightide line. Turned her head to look our way, then resumed her work. Two cubs playing on the driftwood behind her. *What should we do?* I asked Y. He said, *Just wait.* So we did—thirty or forty minutes, until she gathered the cubs and they returned to the forest.

II. *Archive*

Anthropogenic activity is now recognised as having profoundly and permanently altered the Earth system, suggesting we have entered a human-dominated geological epoch, the 'Anthropocene'. To formally define the onset of the Anthropocene, a synchronous global signature within geological-forming materials is required. Here we report a series of precisely-dated tree-ring records from Campbell Island (Southern Ocean) that capture peak atmospheric radiocarbon (14C) resulting from Northern Hemisphere-dominated thermonuclear bomb tests during the 1950s and 1960s. The only alien tree on the island, a Sitka spruce *(Picea sitchensis),* allows us to seasonally-resolve Southern Hemisphere atmospheric 14C, demonstrating the 'bomb

---

```
dynamics, personally. Keynes was perhaps an idealist. there
are also a range of performative theories out there eg if
we stop acting as capitalists it will go away. that is also
at the core of Gibson-grahams post-capitalist politics …
```
He gives up and phones me, just as I'm texting back to ask if by realist he means materialist—as in the limits to growth, if growth stopped around 1972. The conversation ranges: an impromptu lecture on capitalism, an offer of a bookshelf of books—*I'm basically a Marxist structuralist.* He predicts the end of neoliberalism. More internationalist socialist states. There's a locust plague in Kenya, in east Africa. A lot more state presence to ensure sustainable, stable food supply chains. We're just starting to hear from the global South.

peak' in this remote and pristine location occurred in the last-quarter of 1965 (October-December), coincident with the broader changes associated with the post-World War II 'Great Acceleration' in industrial capacity and consumption. Our findings provide a precisely-resolved potential Global Stratotype Section and Point (GSSP) or 'golden spike', marking the onset of the Anthropocene Epoch.

—Abstract, "Global Peak in Atmospheric Radiocarbon Provides a Potential Definition for the Onset of the Anthropocene Epoch in 1965," *Nature,* 19 February 2018

III. *Sequence*

Here we report on the first Sitka spruce chloroplast genome assembled exclusively from *P. sitchensis* genomic libraries prepared using the 10X Genomics protocol. We show that the resulting 124,049 base pair long genome shares high sequence similarity with the related white spruce and Norway spruce chloroplast genomes, but diverges substantially from a previously published *P. sitchensis- P. thunbergia* chimeric genome. The use of reads from high-frequency indices enabled separation of the nuclear genome reads from that of the chloroplast, which resulted in the simplification of the de Bruijn graphs used at the various stages of assembly.

We agree to try to meet in a park one night this week.

Wednesday 15 April 2020, 416.90 ppm. 9:45am
Days of brilliant sunlight. Warm nights. The counter at Johns Hopkins has ticked over: 2 million confirmed cases. Every day is the same. Every evening at 7, the neighbourhood awakens; comes to the windows and the balconies to clap, clatter wooden spoons on pots and pans. Ships' horns. Air horns. Hollers. The nine o'clock gun fires two hours early.
There were 18 wildfires over the long weekend.

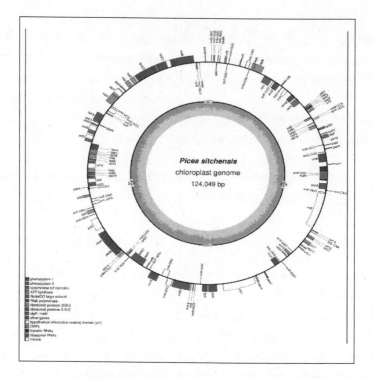

—Lauren Coombe et al. "Assembly of the Complete Sitka Spruce Chloroplast Genome Using 10X Genomics' GemCode Sequencing Data." *PloS ONE*. 15 September 2016.

IV. [   ]

Friday 17 April 2020, 416.91 ppm. 5pm
A wildfire in Squamish.
>An email for M. from the Wildlife Shelter, where she volunteers.
>>Wildlife Rescue has recently made the decision to implement the wearing of masks for on-site staff and volunteers…We are in need of 160 homemade masks, and have 60 accounted for. If you can help us by sewing and donating masks, please reply to this email with the number you are willing to donate. You can find patterns and guidelines here…
>We volunteer to make 20.

blue   blued bluuuue   resonant resin res
                          tympan tam   tam   tam tamp   tamp
    suck whoosh hushhh husshhhhhhhh

   salt   *siit*   *siit siiiiiit*   *tuuxupt* pitch tok tok
        o o   o   tam tam tamp tamp tamp
    suck whooosh   husssssshhhhhh hussshhhhhh
      siit siiiiiit siit sit ka ka   *ka*

    Pandemic style—a bandanna face mask and Dr. Henry pink-and-red Fluevog Oxfords, with her mantra embroidered in the heel: *Be kind, be calm, and be safe.*

Tuesday 21 April 2020, 416.26 ppm
TransLink is laying off 1700 workers and cutting two dozen bus lines, reducing SkyTrain runs. Trump tweeted this morning an Executive Order to close the US to immigrants. The UN is warning starvation is a risk for a quarter billion people unless immediate action is taken: **GLOBAL HUNGER COULD BECOME THE NEXT BIG IMPACT OF THE PANDEMIC.** I send the report to N. He texts back, `yeah, I am worried about safety systems not working. Widespread abandonment of refugees, too.`

II. *PACIFIC SALMON*
(Oncorhynchus)

Scientists have documented more than 12,000 species worldwide that are experiencing range shift—everything from fish to bees to caribou to grasses to berries to trees. "We're literally living through a redistribution of life on Earth," said Gretta Pecl, a marine ecologist at the University of Tasmania and lead author on a recent study of range shift in the journal Science. Pecl said the way this is playing out, in broad strokes, is that in the Northern Hemisphere, plants and animals are moving north, while in the Southern Hemisphere, they're moving south. ...Ultimately, these species are seeking what scientists call climate change "refugia"—areas where they can survive at a time of environmental instability.

— How climate change is leading to 'a
redistribution of life on Earth,'
—CBC Radio, 25 July 2020

1.

I don't know a lot about salmon, only that they undergo a sea change—flesh reddening, darkening blueback to crimson, scarlet, as their bodies thicken and are saturated with carotenoids. Cyclic return up the Fraser after their dark salt wintering. Hooked jaw, incisors split their gums. Translucent

---

VANDU helped some homeless DTES residents to occupy Lord Strathcona Elementary over the weekend for shelter and access to washrooms and running water.
    US oil price fell to -$40 a barrel.

Wednesday 22 April 2020, 415.49 ppm. Earth Day
UN: CORONAVIRUS PANDEMIC 'WILL CAUSE FAMINE OF BIBLICAL PROPORTIONS'
Emails and petitions calling for a green transition.
Something comforting about photographs of wild animals taking over urban spaces—jackals, raccoons, peahens, grey langurs, Sika deer, goats.

scales scorched red. Magnetic cues yield to chemical signatures. As they swim home, they begin to starve.

2.

A. decided to throw a solstice party on her houseboat on Westham Island and asked everyone to write something about the river. After dinner, we went outside into the dock across from this old cannery and she projected Judy's montage of the Fraser Canyon north of Lytton to Boston Flats or thereabouts—trestle bridge, salmon's red-stained flesh, sere land. Again, again, in a loop over a shuddering knocking industrial soundtrack. Everyone climbed out around the water onto different docks and passageways and, as dusk fell, having been called to choreograph, I pointed at people in turn and they would read a line or two; or I pointed at 2 or 3 at once or at everyone, so there might be 2 or 3 voices, or 10, all talking the Fraser. Judy's husband Brian had eaten Kent's soup made out of nuts—at dinner Brian had said, *this soup is so good,* and Kent said, *the secret is you grind the fuck out of the nuts*—at which Brian blanched and gently pushed the bowl away, being allergic to almonds. So Brian felt like puking. Judy sat cross-legged near me right at the water's edge, as a swan came gliding up, and she cried out, *You come at the right time, swan, you're gorgeous!* Fujan wrote a poem to read. I couldn't hear Jacob because he stood so far away. A. read her list of flowers and things she'd been watching the past year in the marshlands. S., N.'s new girlfriend, was maybe feeling a little quiet but said a few things about the co-op farm she runs in Richmond. Y. had written

---

Tuesday 28 April 2020, 415.93 ppm
Total Confirmed Cases: 3, 061, 521
Total Deaths: 212,083
N. sends me Bill Reese's assessment of the new Michael Moore film, *Planet of the Humans*:

Gibbs/Moore—and the subsequent criticism I have seen—all miss a more important point: Even if renewables were 'the answer'—even if techno-industrial capitalist society succeeds in contriving any cheap plentiful substitute for fossil fuels—it would be catastrophic. Without a sea-change in expansionist values and our anthropocentric/

about the sockeye's 4-year life cycle. N., as always a bit contrarian, had written his piece just before the soup, in between jars of red wine, so when I pointed at him, he shouted, *What do I do? What do I talk about?* Someone called out, *Your lines! Your lines!*

OK, he said, *I got my lines.*

3.

There is so much to say about the Fraser. Say something! Sieze the
    moment and—

    The list of flowers and things in the marshlands over
one year—
apple blossom
      St. John's Wort
          single roses
             irises new grasses
                white yarrow scotch broom

Between 2 and 28 million sockeye return to the Fraser every year
to spawn. The average is 9.8 million. The return is cyclical, with a peak
                  every 4 years

---

instrumentalist approach to the natural world, humans would simply use the energy bounty to complete their dismemberment of Earth.

N. is more sanguine and says he is a techno-optimist about our ability as a species to produce beautiful 'things' that are ethical and ecologically benign. We can make bicycles, poems, living buildings; grow plants and trees from seeds.

A. texts me. We talked by Zoom the other day, after she finished submitting her artist grant applications to the Canada Council. All of her projects now focus on the delta, its flora and birds. She has created a bird conservation institute at her university and made a flag for her houseboat
    speaking with a local bird scientist about western sand-
   pipers (they arrive soon, please come see them): i think

purple loosestrife killdeer

They travel through Georgia Strait
at about 45 km a day.

white yarrow scotch broom yellow tansy

Seize the moment and say something! There is so much to say about the Fraser!

The soil from the silt from the Fraser River

lupins chamomile dry brown yarrow

the river is important. I would usually prefer it if people would understand the ecosystem

They travel at about 45 km a day

Under the river, into the tunnel   on the

Half the sockeye return through Johnston Strait   *little brown mushrooms*
and south   through Georgia Strait.

I would usually prefer it if people would understand the ecosystem
in which they live and

I listen and watch

Half return through a southern route of Juan de Fuca strait. They return

purple loosestrife

---

they make the world, in their strange forming shapes, telling the waves how to be white and the islands how to make their island shapes. Elizabeth, the scientist, replies that from a trophic perspective the sandpipers do this, as they take very tiny organisms and convert these to food for themselves -- mammals -- while most birds eat other larger things on the food chain, insects and mammals. so the eagle who is seen as the top of the food chain isn't doing as much making, moving energy only from mammal to mammal state. the sandpiper is moving energy all the way from say an algae to mammal state.

The river is doing a lot! It runs from the caribou mountains and other places
new grasses   white yarrow

It supports many salmon and First Nations
purple loosestrife killdeer goldenrod clover lupin

They return between June and October
I listen and watch
They leave the Fraser between May and July

They winter off the coast in the gulf of Alaska and summer further off shore

I saw the river 4 times today as I rode my bicycle over
the Pattullo Bridge,
the Connector Bridge,
the Alex Fraser bridge and then
ripe blackberry dry brown yarrow dandelions

once I was in Tsawassen, back on River Road
They winter off the coast in the Gulf of Alaska and
summer further off shore

tiny white flowers

I like this. Everything converges, matter and energy and making. But still, I'm feeling pretty blue.

Saturday 2 May 2020, 417.37 ppm
Y. and I went into Camosun bog yesterday. The rain held off. No tree frogs—Y. said he's only been hearing them at night these last few days. Lay down on the boardwalk by the flowering bog laurel—dark pink bells—and watched the orange bumble bees gathering nectar and pollen. They grasp the blossoms with their legs and their fuzzed weight pulls the flower down over top of them like a bonnet. I read somewhere that the vibrations from their buzzing make the pollen fall onto

I saw the river 1, 2, 3, 4 times today. I have never swum in the Fraser

They spend 2 years in the Pacific and mostly return at 4 years old, hence
                                        the 4-year cycle

I saw the river

  The land that I farm is made by the Fraser River   It was here before us

hawthorne mountain ash tall grasses chamomile
      St. John's wort yellow tansy dry brown grasses

Between 2 and 28 million sockeye return to the Fraser every year
to spawn. The average is 9.8 million
                                    It was here before us
            yellow tansy dry brown grasses

    The return is cyclic

---

them. These ones were belted coppery orange, smaller than the larger black and yellow bumble bees—they were there too, some zigzagging over the forest floor, then digging—I don't know what for. Y. said the bumble bees don't sting. I used my loupe to look at the moss—I don't know the names yet, except for sphagnum, which has many varieties. All the white patches in the bog—Y. said they were drying up in the heat, but we had rain a day or two ago, and I picked up a piece of sphagnum that had come loose; it felt silken, plump with rainwater. The boggers had spread out two large sheets of gardening fabric over newly transplanted sphagnum in a trench that Y. said he'd helped dig out last year. Other mosses like tiny emerald stars. Thousands of sporophytes. And ruby tips of fruiting lichen.

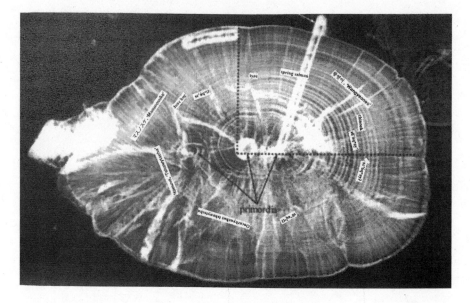

4.

The other day I read a salvaged article in *Hakai* magazine called "Salmon Trees," from May 2000, about the salmon-coastal rainforest nitrogen cycle. It goes like this—a wild red-headed evolutionary biologist studying stick-lebacks on Haida Gwaii found, deep in the forest, *hundreds of snaggle-toothed jaws, spiky ribs and clear, cartilaginous medallions—the circular gill covers of salmon.* So he threw on an ancient green oilskin like a crazed Sir Lancelot and began a quest to figure out how they got there. The writer goes with him and his companions into the estuary and then a river by

---

Later. Back from searching for tree frogs—*Pseudacris regilla*—in a section of the forest that Y. helped clear of Himalayan blackberry. Sticks of alder and red osier dogwood plunged through burlap squares in a jigsaw pattern across the cleared site. And then further back, a few pools of still rainwater, where we'd heard them singing several weeks ago. Looking under leaves, rotting wood—lots of pill bugs, centipedes, slugs—of all colours and sizes. Gently replaced. Sifting through leaves at the water's edge. Sulphurous decay—that's the methane being released, said Y.—anaerobic decomposition. Steady pulse of rain. Y. caught one—years of frog hunting as a boy at summer camp in Michigan—held it out to me in gloved hands and I took it in mine, which were bare. She was small, but

night, which is when the bears come out to feed on the returning salmon—waters thick with noctilucta, chum shooting past their zodiac like stars, *fish scribbling the water with light.* How to measure N-15, rare isotope of Nitrogen—absorbed by salmon in their dark ripening in the Pacific Ocean, now come home to spawn. Their bodies torn and scattered through streams like veins and other bodies; N-15 dispersed by shit and spoor and decayed flesh breeds maggots, feeds birds, fattens bears, grows trees, which nurse the salmon roe.

5.

So after the river dialogue, everyone climbed back inside the houseboat to warm up with tea and coffee and more wine and whiskey, and Jacob had made a poppyseed cake that A. sliced and shared around. Y. had left by then on his bike to catch a bus at the Ladner exchange. Brian still looked ill. S. had fallen asleep, curled up against N. and he looked happier than I'd seen him in a long time. He wasn't going to budge. A. had planned a second act and had set up one of her beautiful old 1950s projectors outside, because she works a lot with light in her art, and had projected a slide she'd made of blades of grass in a clear light—clean like ice or glass—onto the cannery wall; and the idea was we'd read some poetry, but it was late and somehow the moment had passed. Kent brought down his guitar and played a few songs to patch us over to the night and the end of the party. It was way past midnight when we crossed the truss bridge, me, Fujan, N. and S.—her folding bike wedged between them as I drove them home along the River Road.

---

too large and passive to be a tree frog. I could feel her toes grip my palm, see the near translucent speckled cream skin of her sides fill with air. Brownish hood, black eye mask, almost gold around the eyes. Reddish legs. Y. suggested she was a northern red-legged frog—*Rana aurora.* She hopped down onto the mat of decaying leaves. Y. scooped her up and placed her back where he had found her in the watery hollow of a fallen tree's root ball.

Sunday morning, 3 May 2020, -- ppm (data too variable)
And last night, Y. found a tree frog in a little pond just off the trail. *Pseudacris regilla*—false or pseudo-sharp—a reference to the sharpness of the head. But

12. Common Raven
(Corvus corax)

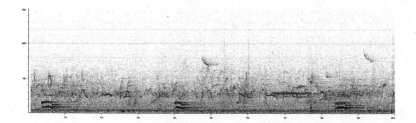

49.3657 latitude, -122.6345 longitude. Widgeon Creek, British Columbia
2019-06-24 13:00 Raven, sonogram, recorded from a canoe.
—https://www.xeno-canto.org/484153

A kind of knocking call, like water dripping into a still pool.
Or a tap on hollowed wood, *tok tok*. Clicks and wing snaps.
Crrruk tuk kluk-kluk kaaa kraaw   quoork quork
wonk-wonk   croooooook   kraa kraa kraaa

I wanted to see ravens, so we climbed the Old Strachan trail

---

to distinguish it from the genus Acris. *Regilla*—splendid, regal; formerly *Hyla regilla—Hyla*, tree. And at some point, *pacifica,* peace-making. *Hyla pacifica* sounds right, but taxonomy gives it a different name. Tiny, loud, and nocturnal. *Crek crek creeeeek.* The rain had stopped and there was moonlight, but we also wore headlamps. Much tinier than *Rana aurora*, and squirmy. Y. passed him to me—like a flicker of breath in my hands. Then he slipped back into the pond and swam to the centre. *Creek crek creeeeeek.* Caught the gleam of a raccoon's eyes at the pond's edge, disappeared. Much further off, deeper in—sounds of voices, a drinking party. Lots of wild creatures in the forest past midnight.

where it branches off the Baaden Powell, past the Hollyburn giant—
thousand-year elder, trail narrowing to a stream bed of roots and
water-smoothed stone, into mist and a thin scree of snow. Some blueberries—
their leaves scarlet. Stripped Sitka mountain ash. A clutch of red berries.
Yellow cedar. Heathers. The tarns were just beginning to ice up.
Y. climbs like a mountain goat, so I trailed behind.
The mist tamped sound. No wind, no birds. A trickle of water. Tap
of my hiking poles. My breath. My steps. My breath. My breath.

I saw Y. first, in the clearing, then torn fuselage. Unexpected,
even though I knew it was there, the debris field recording
the jet's impact—shredded mesh, scorched metal,
roots, bolts, moss, teal wires, pink, blue—a strange tube lichen
fruiting from rusted earth. *These are the remains*
of a Canadian forces T33 trainer, which crashed on Nov 23 1963,
killing 2. Do not take anything. It was the height of the Cold War
and they were flying blind.

Ravens use tools, possess a theory
of mind, plan for the future, speak, mourn, remember.
In the first stories, Raven brings light, fresh water, and fire
to the world. Discovers man in a clam shell. Woman in a chiton.
Frees the sun and the moon, scatters stars. Is a maker,
a transformer, a trickster, a dreamer; dreams of a fire, is scorched
by the flames. *The whole world was burning.*

Tuesday 5 May 2020, 416.44 ppm

PANDEMIC GARDENING: SUPPLYING THE SEEDS

"Some companies have run out of inventory, others have temporarily shut down
their sites to catch up on orders, some have prioritized seed for commercial
farmers over home gardeners in order to support food security," said Stephanie
Hughes, an Atlantic Canadian program manager for Seedchange. Her non-
profit teams up with small farmers to save, share and breed new seeds, amongst
other agricultural extension work. Seeds are a passionate topic for farmers and
a relatively small group of home garden enthusiasts. Normally, that's it. They
get together for Seedy Saturdays in Bridgewater and Truro in February and
March to sell and trade seeds while dreaming of spring. "COVID-19 has

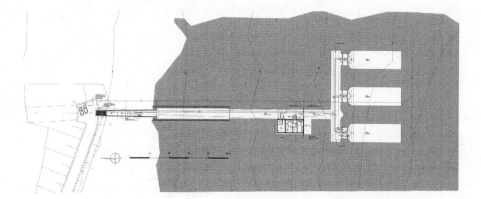

demonstrated to us is that we're not in a good position when disasters strike
with our seed availability," said Hughes. That wasn't a surprise to the seed com-
munity. But it is to the rest of us who just thought we'd plant a garden this
year because of the pandemic and all. Dark galaxy, Wentzell tomato, ground
cherry—those who cherish things that grow tend to be poetic types.
I planted my tomato seedlings yesterday. Also 5 sunflowers on tall stems. Basil—
all grown from seed. Then panicked and rushed out last night to cover them all
with plastic bags in case the temperature dropped too low overnight. Also planted
nursery-bought purple coneflowers, Icelandic poppies, a chocolate lily, near the
wildflowers I scattered a month ago, all for the bees. The arugula, spinach, beets,

13. SILENE STENOPHYLLA
(Svalbard Seed Vault)

The last time I flew to Edmonton, I spent a day working in the Centennial Centre for Interdisciplinary Science and thinking about poetry, about writing a long poem called *Seeds*. Y. had gone to the Northern Forestry Centre to work on his baseline report on the boreal. I was feeling raw in the April light, and free, and kind of blue.

arhar dal

mountain blueyed grass

okra

common timothy

zombie pea

meadow foxtail

cayenne pepper

There's an opening, when I write a poem, like in a dream when you find a room in your home you've never seen before. I space out a bit, but I'm paying attention on a broadband wavelength, unhooked from myself—untethered. And the opening is in my chest, between my breastbone and spine. I'm resonant. I'm clear. And the opening is in language—little mirrors stitched in flesh. Lenticels. Eyes. On the plane, I'd been thinking of blueprints and the *Ecologist's* 1972 *Blueprint for*

---

radishes I planted from seed 2 weeks ago have all popped up. From past years, all the herbs—rosemary, chives with purple blossoms still furled in the bud, lemon balm, spearmint—maybe. Some I forget and just go by smell. The two blueberries and alpine strawberries in blossom. Raspberry canes and grape vine leafing out. Leaks that wintered over. Red chard. Bitter red-veined sorrel.

Thursday 7 May 2020, -- ppm (data too variable)
I heard the so far most perfect description of Sars-CoV-2, as emblem of our future: "surveillance, monopolies, automation, telecommuting, next-generation warfare, UBI, the future of work, the retail apocalypse, online

Kentucky bluegrass

kikuyu grass

sicklefruit

fenugreek

alfalfa

toothed medick

blackeyed pea

rivet wheat

fescue

mung bean

scarlet runner

china aster

ceylon spinach

red clover

buckhorn

Survival. That I'd write a series of blueprints, schemata; of human artefacts and other organisms that expressed resilience, that might survive whatever devastation we've unleashed, whatever is coming down. Blueprints became seeds I gathered. Words. Scraps of ideas.

Silene stenophylla, a type of arctic campion that bloomed in the Pleistocene, resurrected by Russian scientists from 32,000-year-old seeds discovered in a squirrel's den near the Kolyma.

One gram of DNA can hold 455 exabytes of data.

The Reed-Solomon code corrects for reading errors.

The original seed banks were jars and baskets and woven pouches women could wear.

---

dating, anti-Vaxxers, the student debt crisis, supply chain vulnerability, green tech and climate change, urban homelessness, college equivalency certificates, biohacking, the retreat from globalisation, collapse of mainstream journalism, Chinese ascendance, social engineering, Saudi monetization and the move away from fossil fuels in the Kingdom, inclusive stake holding, political realignment and the problem of gerontocracy and the end of naïve capitalism underpinned by New Chicago style economics....you know that tired tech expression, 'the future is already here, it just isn't evenly distributed'? Well this virus is accelerating that unifying future that was already headed

plantain	The Beauty of Loulan, her desiccated body preserved in the Taklamakan, along the old silk road. A woven pouch to carry seeds found buried at her side.
rosary pea	
catchu tree	
orange wattle	Red okra seeds harvested by the Cherokee in Tennessee. Slipped into glass tubes and mailed to Svalbard.
gum arabic	
umbrella thorn	
crookneck squash	A 2000-year-old birch basket found at the Ollie site on the Canadian Plateau, that is, ancestral land of the Tsilhqot'in, Dakelh, Secwepemc, and Upper Nlaka'pomux, was found containing seeds of Saskatoon and raspberry, tiny fragments of charcoal, blades of grass, salmonid bones.
bottle gourd	
roseli	
gold of pleasure	
sunn hemp	
Abyssinian mustard	*Pinus sylvestris* and *Picea abies* collected from Norwegian forests.
uala	Seeds packed in dark magenta crates, delivered from North Korea to deposit in the vault.
bambarra groundnut	

---

our way across the board and recapitulating that moment where agent Kujan drops the Kobayashi coffee mug in The Usual Suspects *film."*
–Eric Weinstein, quoting his partner, the economist Pia Malaney, in episode 31 of The Portal.
N. sends me an article on citizenship for bees:

"Pollinators were the key," says Edgar Mora, reflecting on the decision to recognise every bee, bat, hummingbird and butterfly as a citizen of Curridabat during his 12-year spell as mayor. "Pollinators are the consultants of the natural world, supreme reproducers and they don't charge for it. The plan to convert every street into a biocorridor and every

koa haol

vegetable marrow

Natal indigo

sea clover

slim amarinth

prairie sunflower

Egyptian riverhemp

Chilean tarweed

wild tantan

radish

Irish potato

blue panic

Jamestown weed

Arctic blackberry

thimbleberry

salmonberry

madder

Seeds packed in dark magenta crates, delivered from North Korea to deposit in the vault.

Seeds a dozen scientists died defending in the siege of Leningrad.

As much as *75% of global crop diversity exists outside the big institutional seed banks and is held instead by some of the world's most marginal farmers, most of them women.*

Landrace: *a cultivated, genetically heterogeneous variety that has evolved in a certain ecogeographical area, and is therefore adapted to the edaphic and climatic conditions and to its traditional management and uses. Despite being considered by many to be inalterable, landraces have been and are in a constant state of evolution …*

When the Taliban seized power in Afghanistan, they poured seeds onto the ground in Jalalabad and Ghazni to steal the plastic bottles that held them.

---

neighbourhood into an ecosystem required a relationship with them." The move to extend citizenship to pollinators, trees and native plants in Curridabat has been crucial to the municipality's transformation from an unremarkable suburb of the Costa Rican capital, San José, into a pioneering haven for urban wildlife. Now known as "Ciudad Dulce"— Sweet City—Curridabat's urban planning has been reimagined around its non-human inhabitants. Green spaces are treated as infrastructure with accompanying ecosystem services that can be harnessed by local government and offered to residents. Geolocation mapping is used to target reforestation projects at elderly residents and children to ensure they benefit from air pollution removal and the cooling effects that the

blood sage

winter savoury

common ru

bitter dock

apple of Peru

Peruvian groundcherry

quinoa

Chinese pear

New Jersey tea

beet

borage

Topeka purple coneflower

charlock

mustard

sea kale

horn of plenty

weeping lovegrass

The Svalbard Seed Bank, carved into the permafrost on Longyearbyen—half year in twilight, half in darkness—a backup to the backups. In May 2017 it flooded due to permafrost melt. No seeds were harmed.

Staff at the International Centre for Agricultural Research in the Dry Areas in Aleppo smuggled seeds out in jars and bags as the civil war drew near.

Two undergraduate students at the University of Maribor in Slovenia thought one day, *Why can't we put all the data in the history of mankind in one stone, near spruce or oak ... and that was the click.*

They meant not stone, but seed—like spruce or meadowrue, that could reproduce itself and grow.

(The opening is metaphor. Little mirrors stitched into flesh.)

That day in Edmonton, in the cavernous foyer an articulated plesiosaur—cretaceous sea creature—

---

trees provide. The widespread planting of native species underscores a network of green spaces and biocorridors across the municipality, which are designed to ensure pollinators thrive.
    –The Guardian, Wed. 29 April

Wednesday 13 May 2020, 416.61 ppm
We hiked up Brothers trail yesterday afternoon to Blue Gentian Lake. It was still mostly frozen and covered in several feet of snow. Pools of dark icy water emerging at its edges, filled with algae and sphagnum moss. The hike begins on an old logging road with abandoned equipment at its edges, a skid road, regrown clear-cut—no understory, just a litter of rust-coloured needles. Ascent to selectively

apple mint

wild mint

catmint

spearmint

coalberry

common comfrey

Aztec marigold

feverfew

red huckleberry

common tansy

holy basil

meadowrue

floated in 21st century light. I took notes in a laboratory notebook with turquoise numbered pages, which I'd bought on a previous trip here, in a February snowstorm. I am still using it, taking notes on this dangerous human experiment.

I can't get through. I think I come close—a glimpse, which closes up. Like the first moment of a deep wound when clear fluid wells, before dark blood pools and obscures. Or the artist's rough charcoal sketch—somehow closer to the thing in itself than the finished work.

Against this: human consciousness may have evolved to be epistemologically incapable of perceiving the world as it is; we see only a mediating interface, the world is a mathematical code. As language is a code. But metaphor is an opening, is the beautiful cell. Ground lens. Charcoal. Raspberry seed. Salmonid bone.

---

cut forest—mossy stumps of old growth scarred with springboard notches, more cedar, more understory, beautiful old giants quilted with moss. The higher we climbed, the earlier the season—salmon berry unfurling papery dark pink blooms, then fewer, then pink twists of paper, then leaf buds as patches of snow appeared and grew, mist rising. Like walking back in time, before logging, before the virus, early spring morning of the world.

Saturday 16 May 2020, -- ppm (data too variable)
At Y.'s. Lay on the boardwalk at Camosun bog yesterday afternoon in the sun. A sea of pinks from the bog laurel, sun-bleached, will give way to white blooms of

Labrador tea. Sphagnum moss. A tiny sundew. Tasted the crumpled papery tip of a bracken fern and soft tips of grand fir, like sunlight and lime.

Thursday 21 May 2020, 417.10 ppm
Just as we begin the second phase of returning to a 'new normal,' the news is flowered with warnings of a second wave to hit in the Fall. Enjoy this temporary respite. Conspiracy theories also viral. Antisemitic. Anti-vax. Alt-right. Sars-Cov2 was engineered by the Chinese as a bioweapon, which escaped from the level 4 virus lab in Wuhan. Sars-Cov2 was engineered as a bioweapon by the US or by Russia and deliberately released in Wuhan to disguise its origin. Sars-Cov2

14.

⊗

(Getting deeper)

327.45 ppm

I begin with 1972, year 11,972 of the Holocene era, the year *The Ecologist* published *A Blueprint for Survival* to warn that we were running out of time. My mom in a yellow tank top and bell-bottom jeans grips my sister by her left hand, me by the other. We're dressed in identical play suits, apple-green sleeveless tops and sky-blue shorts. I'm barefoot, with a turquoise floral kerchief. I can feel the heat baked into the granular sidewalk, grit under my toes. From the front door of our house on east 56th, an entrance we never use except for guests, there's a clear view of Mount Baker. We always take the side entrance—through the mudroom where my mom stands for hours by the hinged window, pinning laundry with wooden pegs to the line, reeling it out to flap in the breeze, reeling it back again, sterilized by the sun. The snap of white sheets folded into squares. A fresh scoured smell of earth and wind. This is my earliest memory.

---

was engineered by Bill Gates who will conveniently 'discover' a vaccine, which, when administered, will simultaneously inject a microchip into every human on the planet.

Friday 22 May 2020, 416.57 ppm

ANTARCTICA IS TURNING GREENER AS A RESULT OF CLIMATE CHANGE. In summer, parts of Antarctica are turning bright green as algae bloom across the surface of the melting snow. Now, scientists have created the first large-scale map of microscopic algae on the Antarctic

The average CO_2 in the atmosphere that year, measured at the observatory on Mauna Loa, is 327.45 parts per million. In the UK, the editors of *The Ecologist* are writing,

> Radical change is both necessary and inevitable, because the present increase in human numbers and per capita consumption, by disrupting ecosystems and depleting resources, are undermining the very foundations of survival.

335.42 ppm

We live in a small bungalow in a working class, immigrant neighbourhood in East Vancouver. Rust-coloured shag carpet. Avocado green fridge and stove. Beige Bakelite telephone attached to the kitchen wall—the cord is long and coiled. Later, as a teenager, I can pull it around the corner to crouch at the top of the basement stairs and talk with friends. We wash the dishes by hand. Outside in the backyard there's a large open compost heap, where we toss vegetable peelings, leftovers, scraps, grass cuttings. Mom turns it with the pitchfork and when it is cooked, works it back into the garden. Grows geraniums, tomatoes. Two metal tins for the garbage, with lids that clang shut, are placed in the lane every week. My sister and I walk to school, find the thick fuzzy black and orange caterpillars I never see anymore, ride our bikes around the neighbourhood all summer, are called home at dusk.

---

peninsula, published on 20 May in Nature Communications (1). The algae, which provide an important terrestrial carbon sink, are likely to spread across the continent as global temperatures continue to increase.

Monday 25 May 2020, 418.04 ppm
Sightings of humpback whales near Deep Cove, and in Vancouver Harbour. J.B. MacKinnon describes how less than a century ago this would have been an everyday occurrence, "grey and even humpback whales—the species famous for its beautiful, mournful underwater songs—were an ordinary presence off Vancouver's shore."

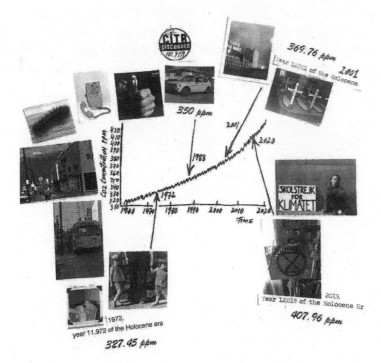

342.53 ppm

Every summer, we load up the Volvo and drive the Hope-Princeton to Penticton for two weeks at the Bowmont Motel. We listen to mixed tapes: Itchycoo Park, If I Could Save Time in a Bottle, American Pie. *Can music save your mortal soul, And can you teach me how to dance, real slow?* We swim in the pool during lightning storms. Burn, peel. I read Shakespeare—*Romeo*

Monday 30 May 2020, 416.48 ppm
There have been protests across the US overnight over the killing of George Floyd, who kept repeating, *I can't breathe, I can't breathe,* as a police officer kneeled on his throat for 9 minutes. Minneapolis—where he died. Detroit, Atlanta, Portland, Louisville, Los Angeles, Houston, New York, Lincoln, Nebraska, Oakland, California, Washington, DC. They tried to hurl bottles and bricks over the White House gates. Trump tweeted that if they'd have breeched the wall, they "would have been greeted with the most vicious dogs, and most ominous weapons, I have ever seen." The protestors' slogan is, *I can't breathe.* Trump is scheduled to fly to Cape Canaveral today for the test flight of Space X, financed by a billionaire who builds gigabyte factories in the desert that may or may not supply renewable energy; and who just

and Juliet—for the first time, surprised to find that it's poetry. The motel owner's teenage son takes us for a ride on his motorcycle. I hold my body against a boy's hard back for the first time. The blue-neon light outside the office crackles and zaps bugs. For years, Dad works as a clerk in a provincial liquor store, member of the BCGEU. Works nights doing stock taking. Goes on strike. Takes exams to become an assistant manager. Mom, a keypuncher before I was born, takes part-time jobs while we're in school: receptionist, typist, garden shop clerk, housecleaner.

344.16 ppm

I learn to drive stick in a Honda Civic. The year before I graduate high school, the Brundtland Report appears: *Our Common Future.* It's 1987, year 11,987 of the Holocene Era. The average ppm of CO_2 in the atmosphere is 344.16. In my human geography class, we study the Green Revolution. Its aftermath. The World Bank. Megaprojects like hydro dams. GMOs. We go on a field trip to the Brittania Mines, Shannon Falls, Squamish. All I remember of this trip is the pouring rain, twilight at noon—the heavy comforting weight of the oil skin slicker draped over my shoulders by my teacher, who must have thought I looked cold. The Intergovernmental Panel on Climate Change is created a year later, and we lurch unsteadily into the future. James Hansen warns the US Congress, *The greenhouse effect has been detected and it is changing our climate now.* The CO_2 in the atmosphere is 350 ppm.

---

named his seventh son, by his girlfriend Grimes, XAE, A-Xii, aka 'Little X.' COVID-19 cases surging in India, Brazil, Russian, the US, Afghanistan, the UK. This is still the first wave. This could all be a page out of *Radio Free Albemuth*.

Thursday 4 June 2020, 416.76 ppm
Second week of protests. Trump channeling Nixon circa 1968. Tear gas and riots upstaging peaceful mass protests across the US. More egregious recorded examples of police brutality and violence. Curfews. Police with riot gear and tanks. Pepper spray. Rubber bullets. Antifa. Boogaloos. Everything intense and magnified, amplified, by months of quarantine, loss of livelihood, disproportionate loss of black lives to COVID-19, the rising heat. Mostly peaceful protests here.

354.29 ppm

I study literature at UBC but spend every waking minute at the student radio station, CiTR., in the sweet scent of album sleeves, in A-control, in C-control. The Sugar Cubes. Billy Bragg. REM. *Tell me with the Rapture and the reverent in the right, right, you vitriolic, patriotic, slam fight, bright light, feeling pretty psyched.* The engineer takes me up to the top of Gage Tower one Christmas Eve to see the antenna that broadcasts our signal at 101.9 megaHerz over the glittering ocean at the cliff edge. My boyfriend sinks into darkness, runs into the endowment lands that surround the university, into the forest, until he can't live with himself any longer and runs in front of a car. For a long time, the world is thin and stark like a film negative or an X-ray. Even the brightest sunlit day is shadow and void. I don't believe in words for a long time. I stop paying attention.

369.76 ppm

After several years working in a biomedical library, I move to Montreal to do my PhD, September 1999. I miss the Battle for Seattle, just as I did the War in the Woods. I live in a 5 ½ on Côte des Neiges, with a glimpse from the balcony across the divide to Westmount, down to the mercurial river and the neon *Farine Five Roses* sign. I walk up the mountain, behind the apartment, to the Lac aux Castors, along Avenue des Pins, past the home of Trudeau père, to my seminars at McGill. Montreal is a surreal cutout. My father dies; we had no warning. The ice

---

Everything is interconnected but fractured. We can't seem to come together, and the earth is burning. SARS-Cov2 is not evolving quickly enough to have been transmitted directly from bat to pangolin to human; it is already adapted to its human host. It has probably been engineered, a chimera—created from a corona bat virus found in Yunnan, a spike protein from a pangolin that allows it to bind to human cells, a 12-letter furin cleavage site to finetune the lock:

> Nikolai Petrovsky and colleagues at Flinders University in Australia have found that SARS-Cov-2 has a higher affinity for human receptors than for any other animal species they tested, including pangolins and horseshoe bats. He suggests that this could have happened if the virus was being cultured in human cells, adding that 'We can't exclude the possibility that this came from

sets in, and the cold. My sister flies out for New Year's Eve, and we mourn. A new century begins.

John Bellamy Foster is scouring Marx for a seminal book on ecology:

> trying to lay out a consistent naturalism, humanism, and materialism, 'man is directly a natural being...equipped with natural powers...on the other hand, as a natural corporeal, sensuous, objective being he is a suffering, conditioned and limited being, like animals and plants'.

There are protests and teddy bear catapults at the 3rd Summit of the Americas in Quebec City. I'm pregnant with my daughter. A visiting aunt who is considering becoming a nun brings us on a tour of the motherhouse of Les Soeurs Grises. We walk the cavernous halls, see the chapel, the crypt. My daughter is born a month later, November 2001. 369.76 ppm. Year 12,001 of the Holocene.

We march in the streets of Montreal. Again. Again. Each time larger. 100,000 strong. Girls draped in blood-soaked white sheets line the boulevards. A boat crowded with the dead sails a ribbon of blue silk strung taut by mourners. The US invades Iraq.

377 ppm—407.96 ppm

I move home to Vancouver, lose track of time. Teach at the University, then the College. Reconnect with N. Meet Y. Read books on the Great Transition. *Desert. Dark Mountain. Climate Leviathan.* In Stockholm, a

---

a laboratory experiment'...Whatever the initial spark, what turned a brush fire into a global conflagration was city life. Viruses have erupted into human beings from contact with nature many times in the past when more of the population lived in rural areas hunted animals for food and foraged in forests for firewood, contact with bats would have been more frequent. But chains of infection in rural villages would have petered out. –Matt Ridley, *The Wall Street Guardian*

FPSE ad hoc climatic committee met via Zoom the other day. At least 2 of us will probably be laid off. Everything stalled—sustainability plans, climate action plans—there's a huge increase in disposables, chemicals, waste. How to frame this moment as a possibility for social and structural change.

getting deeper
15 messages

N██████████ <n██@q████████n>   3 May 2018 at 09:2
To: kim trainor <kimtrainor7@gmail.com>

I don't really know what you know and don't know about ecological politics. My sense is that movements in the 2000s to separate out climate change from broader ecological movements are misguided-- or guided by technocratic policy reformers.

The really key movements are:

(i) in the late 1960s and early 1970s, the emergence of 'deep' green perspectives--- Here is a note on the Ecologists' Blueprint for Survival from 1972. https://theecologist.org/2012/jan/27/ecologist-january-1972-blueprint-survival with a link to the original statement. Bill Rees and his ecological footprint are really in this camp. (His book his cool, read it!). For Climate, the Post Carbon Institute is here.

(ii) this spirals into various forms of 'deep ecology' in the 1980s. The wilderness preservations and the eco-feminists etc.

(iii) but "sustainable development" in the mid 1980s was really a growth of a counter-movement against the 'ecologists' in the name of liberalism. Bruntland report, then 1992 Earth Summit. Bernstein in the Compromise of Liberal Environmentalism really describes this well. You can also look for literature on "ecological modernisation". Essentially, this becomes the 'policy reform'/climate leviathan camp. Most environmental economists, political scientists, legal scholars are in this camp, and there are very well funded studies by the OECD, UNEP, the Stern Review etc. outlining policy proposals. for climate, the IPCC, while it tries to be 'neutral' is more or less in this camp. In the mid 2000s there was a lot of flashy attempts to gain adherents to these perspectives in the US, with the "bright green" types---in some cases it gets very technologically oriented--people like Amory Lovins and Paul Hawken talk of 'green capitalism' which they mean, e.g. a lot of sparkly innovation. Lovins is very smart though, but pragmatic.

(iv) By the 1990s there is a growing "social green" perspective-- found in Murray Bookchin's Social Ecology (while anarchist it was an early entry and was widely read by non-radicals), the rise of "political ecology" as an academic movement, as well as people who start with sustainable development and start to take equity and public participation more seriously. John Robinson's work (he was at UBC for a while) is a good example. "Canada in 2030" is an example of a social democratic version. At times UNEP seems to go this direction. For climate, also look at "Contraction and Convergence" models. Also various labour side "green economy" proposals fit this. Like Van Jones in "Green Jobs" or Klein/Lewis' "The Leap".

(v) By the early 2000s there are a lot of eco-socialists around. Marx's Ecology is the best example of that work. James O'Connor is quite famous too; I can send you articles. I can led you tonnes of books by John Bellamy Foster. Also David Harvey writes in this tradition. Wainright and Mann are kind of poor followers of that, or simply trying to offer a new twist.

Tuesday 9 June 2020, 415.86 ppm. Windy Joe fire lookout

Windy Joe trailhead. Hiked up yesterday. The Windy Joe trailhead is also the northern start of the Pacific Crest Trail. We'd planned to stay the night at a PCT campsite, but there was so much blowdown along the trail—for much of the second half of the trail, having to crawl under fallen trees or climb over them—we decided to try for Windy Joe directly and arrived at dusk. Patches of snow, more as we ascended. The Cascades stretching far in the distance. The hut intact: clean, wood, at all 4 corners secured by metal wires that sing in the wind. Inside there are 2 benches, a shovel, an axe, a broom. A ladder up to the lookout post with the metal finding tool still in place, still working. Mud-green witches' hair hanging from the branches of subalpine pine and floating in the snow we melt for

5-year-old girl stands on the steps of the Swedish parliament holding a sign that reads, *Skolstrejk för Klimatet*. More join her. More. We join her. We gather at City Hall for the climate strike. It's hard to find each other in the crowd. I find N. I can't find my sister. My kids have made a sign, a green painted square with a black symbol, ⊗. Extinction Rebellion has been around for just over a year. Its original demands:

> 1. Government must tell the truth by declaring a climate and ecological emergency, working with other institutions to communicate the urgency for change.
> 2. Government must act now to halt biodiversity loss and reduce greenhouse gas emissions to net-zero by 2025.
> 3. Government must create, and be led by the decisions of, a citizens' assembly on climate and ecological justice.

I've taped Animal to the back of our sign with his arms draped over the front, banging chopsticks on it like a drum. We surge across the Cambie Street bridge. We're 120,000 strong. It takes several hours to move downtown. We meet up with A. Outside the VPL, we stage a die in. It's Friday, 27th September 2019. Year 12,019 of the Holocene Era. 407.96 ppm and rising. XR's symbol is a circumscribed hourglass, the extinction symbol. It announces: we're running out of time.

---

water. Yellow glacier lilies everywhere in bloom. We set up the tent outside; we are using the hut as shelter for cooking and to cache the food. I woke briefly to a gentle sound, like rain, but softer. Woke at 6am to find the blue tent covered in a white blanket of snow. I'm reading *Learning to Die in the Anthropocene: Reflections on the End of a Civilization.*

> For humanity to survive in the Anthropocene, we need to learn to live with and through the end of our current civilization. Change, risk, conflict, strife, and death are the very processes of life, and we cannot avoid them. We must learn to accept and adapt.

There's no signal. No water source beyond the snow. Two fire pits with charred wood. Tomorrow we'll hike down.

Thursday 11 June 2020, 416.53 ppm
An email from N. while I was away with a link to an article in *Resilience*:

'COLLAPSE OF CIVILIZATION IS THE MOST LIKELY OUTCOME':
TOP CLIMATE SCIENTISTS

Schellnhuber, one of the world's leading authorities on climate change,
said that if we continue down the present path "there is a very big risk
that we will just end our civilisation. The human species will survive
somehow but we will destroy almost everything we have built up over
the last two thousand years."

15. HYMENOPTERA
(honey bee, bumblebee, Vespa orientalis)

I.

N. texts me, the poet moves towards the impenetrable
—the sweet honey of darkness, where it simply must be
that meaning lies (others just use lights).
Animalia | Arthropoda | Insecta | Hymenoptera | Apidae and Vespidae.
Dark fuzzed body, orange-belted, opaque. The impenetrable, the sweet.
The packet of seeds sent me by the Wilderness Committee—fleabane daisy,
dwarf godetin, prairie coneflower, lewis flax—instructs,
*Plant seeds in a sunny location after all danger of frost has passed. Cover
with 1/8th soil.* Some need the dark form of phytochrome to germinate.
The queens are emerging from their long winter and search out a new hollow
underground. I saw one yesterday at Mountainview Cemetery, where I met
Lucie as I used to do. Humming. Buzz buzz. Zigzagging, intent, a recce, as
she prowled the grass in bare feet over ribbons of sunken concrete that mark
deaths from a century ago. *Look, look, I'm social distancing with the dead!
Can I borrow a pen?* No. *Because then you'd have to disinfect it?*

Wednesday 17 June, 416.08 ppm
Climate crisis: alarm at record-breaking heatwave in Siberia
Unusually high temperatures in region linked to wildfires, oil spill and
moth swarms.

Thursday 18 June, 415.71 ppm
World has six months to avert climate crisis, says energy expert
The world has only six months in which to change the course of the
climate crisis and prevent a post-lockdown rebound in greenhouse
gas emissions that would overwhelm efforts to stave off climamte ca-
tastrophe, one of the world's foremost energy experts has warned.

Yes—I only brought one pen. *Your laptop?* No. *You can disinfect it.*
No, I can't. *I'm an essential worker.* She steps over her notebook,
flung open on the grass to a page scrawled in Sharpie or black crayon.
But the libraries are closed? *They called me back to Insite but
we can only have six people at a time, instead of 12. It's easier.
It's all a scam.* No, it isn't. *To control the population! Also,
there was no moon landing.* Obviously. A sign at the entrance reads,

**THIS SPACE SHOULD NOT BE USED FOR LEISURE
ACTIVITIES DURING THESE EXCEPTIONAL TIMES.**

But there are no mourners here. Just the two of us, and the dead
at rest. Sleeping. Humming. Buzz, buzz. The impenetrable, the sweet sun
on my back. Lucie is a pale ginger and burns like me. Settles in the shade,
wrapped in her black fur-lined coat. We are working on her manuscript—

*On Keats Island there's no reception / and a few fields cleared
for my waiting. / Once it gets dark, there will be owls / everywhere.*

A bumblebee hovers at my wrist, then moves sideways, zig-
zagging methodically over the uneven grass, driven. I have read
that they live for only one season. Now she has withdrawn
into herself. Blue scatters over the graves.

Wednesday 1 July 2020, 415.35 ppm. Sombrio east, Juan de Fuca trail, 28km marker
Grey sky, swelling sea. *Quork, quork.* Ravens nearby. I think we'll leave today.
Campfires all along the beach last night, again this morning—darker pall of
smoke drifting up into the spruce along the shore. I finished *Learning to Die in the
Anthropocene*. I like Scranton's insistence on the "patient nurturing of the roots
and heirloom varietals of human symbolic life…a practice of active attention, culti-
vation, making and remaking. It is not enough for the archive to be stored, mapped,
or digitized. It must be *worked*." And of digital humans as *Homo lux*—humanity as
collective energy, light swarming across a darkened planet, a geological forcing,
data and flow. We live in networks, webs, and hives, jacked in to remote-con-
trolled devices and autonomous apps, moments of being in time, out of time.

II.

The bees and the wasps are making the world. The bees, the honey bees, the bumble bees, search out voids and hollows—underground, in straw, in hay, in pots, the dark hollows of trees, crevices in stone. The wasps, the hornets, the yellow jackets search out voids and hollows—underground, in trees, under eaves, in abandoned cars and shipping containers, garages and crawl spaces and sheds. The honey bees collect resin from tree buds and mix it with chewed wax and saliva to coat the nest with propolis, which has anti-microbial properties. The hornets strip wood fibres in thin white lines from cedar planks and weathered porches, from oak twigs and the branches and bark of spruce and chestnut and apple and cherry. They chew the wood in their mouths and mix it with saliva and wax to build their papery cells. The queen did this, first to build a petiole; then a single cell; then six, joined to the narrow stalk. The bumble bees are gathering nectar from the wild-flowers, the dandelions, salvia, Russian sage, lavender, chives—all the blue flowering ones. They mix the nectar with enzymes, and as the water evap-orates honey is formed and transformed into wax, which they chew up to make the cells. The wasps are *intuitive architects*. They are building complex papery nests, woven with strips of colour, the colours of the materials they chew: the red cedar, the mint-green porch, threads of a faded pink deck chair. The bees possess *a certain geometrical forethought*. They are using their bodies as measuring tools to build their hexagonal cells. The oriental wasps are harvesting light with their bright-yellow-banded abdomens. With the

No longer individual subjects or discrete objects, we have become vibrations, channelers, tweeters and followers…biologically reactive, easily panicked, all too quickly stirred to hatred.

He feels violence is always necessary, and can achieve good, as well as bad—as in the struggle to free the slaves, the workers' struggles for human rights–only possible because they were coal miners and could stop the flow of energy, as in the civil rights movement. Scranton relies on a salvage paradigm, the need for somehow preserving

not just biological arks, to carry forward endangered genetic data, but also cul-tural arks….The library of human cultural technologies that is our archive, the concrete record of human thought in all languages that comprises the entirety

obscure pigment xanthopterin, they generate chemical energy to dig in the heat of the day. The honey bees are gathering pollen and nectar, trembling. The bumble bees are reading the colours and shapes and patterns of the flowers—the faint pulse of the floral electrical fields—to pollinate the flowers, to gather the pollen and nectar. The bees are making the honey, the royal jelly, the propolis, bee bread, bee brood, and venom. The bees and the wasps are making the world.

---

of our existence as historical beings, is not only the seed stock of our future intellectual growth, but its soil, its source, its womb.
Suck and hush of the tide, all night, in the shelter of a Sitka spruce.

Sunday 12 July 2020, 413.92 ppm. 10am
Sometimes there is a feeling of normality, except for the 6m spacing as we line up outside shops: the plastic shields and face masks on the clerks and restaurant servers, the sudden profusion of temporary outdoor patios or sidewalks, spilled out into the parking lanes. The supply claims have mostly caught up for now with the demand for latex gloves, masks, Isopropyl alcohol, hand sanitizer. But then

16. PACIFIC TREE FROG
(Hyla regilla, Pseudacris regilla)

In the course of his argument, Ortega gains the important insight that each of us is an 'I' not because we each have a special zoological apparatus called 'consciousness,' but because each of us is something, and that something can never be exhausted by conscious introspection any more than by outward description. It follows that every non-human object can also be called an 'I' in the sense of having a definite inwardness that can never fully be grasped.
> —Graham Harman, *A Theory of Everything: Object Oriented Ontology*

Now then, imagine the importance of a language or system of expressive signs whose function was not to tell us about things but to present them to us in the act of executing themselves. Art is just such a language; this is what art does. The esthetic object is inwardness as such—it is each thing as 'I.'
> —José *Ortega* Y. Gasset, "An essay in esthetics by *way* of a preface" (1914)

1. I heard them first, nights in Point Grey, long before I knew their name.

2. In 'human language'—*ribbet, ribbet; shirk-it, shirk-it; kreck-eeck; krrrreck; kreck-ek; krr-r-r-ck; ooh-yeeh* (?!); *rib-bit; crek-ek; cre-ee-ee-eck.*

I turn to the news and some of the US states are in lock down or running out of ICU beds and space in the morgues—Arizona most recently, caught unawares by exponential growth. Trump threatens to withhold funding from schools if they don't reopen in the Fall. Some Republicans proclaim they would die to restart the economy. Are these the long-drawn-out death throes of unfettered capitalism fueled by cheap oil and the need for endless consumption and growth? The headline yesterday: **GLOBAL 'CATASTROPHE' LOOMS AS COVID-19 FUELS INEQUALITY.** *The pandemic has exposed and reinforced deep inequalities across the world, with the true extent yet to be seen, according to a major new report. The crisis in the poorest countries threatens to escalate into a catastrophe as job*

3. Or scientific. *Animalia chordata amphibia anura hylidae pseudacris pseudacris regilla*, formerly *hyla regilla*.

4. *Small but iconic.*

5. In various colours. Qualitative descriptions of frogs 1 through 20: green with brown patches, brown with brown-red tinge, brown with green sides, brown with grey sides, brown with green sides, gray-brown, red back with gold sides, brown with green sides, grey with green fringes, brownish grey, brown with green undertones, brown, brown with grey sides, grayish green with copper tinges, gold with green sides, brown with green sides, green, brown, green.

6. *Smaller than a dime.*

7. I would walk through dark streets, following their sound—the pulse of night.

8. Systole. Diastole. Systole. Diastole. Systole.

9. Of course, the colour preceived is dependent on the visual system specific to the perceiver.

10. **RARE BLUE FROG STRUTS ITS STUFF AT NHM.**
   —*Humboldt State Now*, 6 June 2008

---

losses and food insecurity mount. Drought. Food shortages. Lack of most basic hygiene facilities to wash hands. America thrashes, sickens, and will lash out. More dangerous now than ever.

We spent the afternoon in Malcolm Knapp, in the rain, measuring understory growth in the research forest. It's slow going. Sample square metres to estimate 'herbs'—salmonberry, moss, herb-Robert, deer fern, sword fern, all below 1m in height. A transect line to measure shrubs over 1m—Salmonberry, sword fern, bracken, for the most part. Then a radial sweep to identify and measure trees—all planted in 1999, in various mixes of deciduous and conifer. Mostly alder, paper

11. A rare mutation in its pigment cells—a missing layer of yellow xanthophores—that would transform reflected blue light into green.

12. Blue is rare in animals, *so my eyes said yum.*

13.

14. *Reflectance spectra from the dorsal surface of each frog were measured with a spectraradiometer (Spectrascan model 714) using the standard beam method .... in an otherwise darkened experimental chamber.*

15. They have superior detection of blue light—we think they can see in the dark.

16. As they hunt, prey blurs across their field of vision, like a long exposure film.

17. I would hear them, but I could never see them.

18.

---

birch, cedar, Douglas fir, hemlock. All fairly slim, so that I can still reach my hands around one; not quite one hand around the slimmest alder and birch. The paper birch here aren't white but reddish brown—a coastal variety? When very young, the hemlock and fir look almost like alder with lenticels on the trunk and no grooved bark, so you have to look up to see the needles or leaves—or at least I do. But the cedar always looks like cedar. It rained constantly and the undergrowth was thick in places. A few old cedar stumps, massive old growth, wider than my arms outspread, thick with moss. We managed only plots S, T, and half of Q.

19. *Krr-r-r-rk. Krick-ek.* One. And then another. Another. Singing.

20.
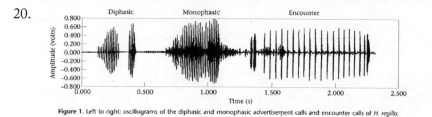

Figure 1. Left to right: oscillograms of the diphasic and monophasic advertisement calls and encounter calls of *H. regilla.*

21.   After the first heavy winter rains in California, *every roadside ditch, every pond, every puddle, every little spot of water has attracted to itself a Tree-toad chorister.* —Gayle Pickwell, *Amphibians and Reptiles of the Pacific States,* 1931

22.   Each male defends his song territory.

23.   This experiment will place each frog against a dark brown or bright green background.

24.   *The following ED equation was used because it allowed us to track color change in a three-dimensional color space:*

$$ED = \sqrt{((a_f - a_c)^2 + (b_f - b_c)^2 + (L_f - L_c)^2)}$$

25.   Its distinctive black eye band looks *somewhat like a mask that a fictional villain might wear.*

Saturday 18 July 2020, 414.17 ppm

JAMES LOVELOCK: 'THE BIOSPHERE AND I ARE BOTH IN THE LAST 1% OF OUR LIVES'Is the virus part of the self-regulation of Gaia?
Definitely, it's a matter of sources and sinks. The source is the multiplication of the virus and the sink is anything we can do to get rid of it, which is not at the moment very effective. This is all part of evolution as Darwin saw it. You are not going to get a new species flourishing unless it has a food supply. In a sense that is what we are becoming. We are the food. I could easily make you a model and demonstrate that as the human population on the planet grew larger and larger, the probability of a virus evolving that would cut back the population

26. A Pacific tree frog will eat *almost anything*: spiders and ants, little beetles, leafhoppers, isopods. *Anything smaller than itself.* Even its own shed skin. They are *voracious predators.*

27. Pacific tree frogs are eaten by: kestrels, herons, egrets, the western territorial garter snake (*Thamnophis elegans*), western red-tailed hawks, belted kingfisher (*Megaceryle alcyon*), raccoons and *Felix domestica*, the domestic house cat.

28. This experiment will test the impact of climate warming and rapid pond drying in *Pseudacris regilla.*

29. *We established experimental ponds in 48 1000-L plastic cattle tanks at the University of British Columbia's Experimental Pond Facility (Vancouver, British Columbia, Canada) in spring 2012.*

30. Recipe for a pond:
>~500L of city water to a depth of 28cm
>2 kg of dried deciduous leaf matter
>1.5L concentrated plankton
>10 μm/L phosphorous as KH_2PO_4
>160 μm/L nitrogen as $NaNO_3$ *mix*

>Add tadpoles.

---

is quite marked. We're not exactly a desirable animal to let loose in unlimited numbers on the planet. Malthus was about right. In his day, when the human population was much smaller and distributed less densely across the planet, I don't think Covid would have had a chance.

Sunday 19 July 2020, 413.86 ppm. 10am
Finished in the research forest yesterday, after five days of surveying until dusk each day. The young hemlock and alder and Douglas fir no longer look the same to me at all. I can tell just by a glance at the bark which it is, as I can whether it is alder or birch. The Douglas fir has blisters, all over and horizontal with the ground, and

31. Sometimes I could not hear them at all. Or, suddenly—

32.

33.

34. *Kr-rrr-rrek. Krik-ek.*

35. *We plotted the hue, lightness, chroma, and color distances against time...*

36. I heard them on a road trip through the Mojave, although I didn't know them.

37. This experiment will measure the impact of road noise on Pacific chorus frog communication.

38. *The recording equipment was comprised of a Sennheiser MKH20 microphone (sensitivity: –32 dB re 1 V/Pa) in a Telinga parabolic directional housing, attached to a Zoom H4n recorder...*

39. The desert singing in the night.

40. From British Columbia to Baha California. From the Pacific Ocean to 10,000 feet above sea level. The Sierra Nevadas. Soda Springs. Nevada.

---

if you press firmly with your thumb the blister pops and a sticky resin oozes out—bitter to the taste but its scent is magnificent, the essence of fir. The hemlock is smoother with stitches when very young. Alder is smooth—perhaps I would glance up to confirm hemlock or alder. Some of the alder in the last plot we surveyed had beautiful eyes, or knots, like a fire brand of the eye of Horus. The birch peels, and the very young skin beneath, gleams copper with lighter, tight stitches.

I'm tattooed with mosquito bites, huckleberry scratches, bruises. Glad we didn't run into any black bears, as there was bear scat everywhere. Although we saw a mother and her 2 cubs, all on their hind legs, at the entrance our first day—watching us as we drove past the open meadow and the picnic table.

Montana. And two frogs taken from Port Coquitlam and released near Port Clements on Haida Gwaii in 1964.

41. *We characterized the anthropogenic and Pacific chorus frog components of each site's soundscape over the course of both breeding seasons by quantifying ambient road noise levels and timing as well as general chorus structure.*

42. On humid spring nights, they sing.

43. They sing.

44. When a female approaches a male, he abandons his song and assumes amplexus. She ferries him on her back to the quiet shallows.

45. *The males will often attempt to mate with any non-vocalizing amphibian that gets too close…not only male Pacific tree frogs, but other species of frogs, and even salamanders…*

46. She lays between 30 and 70 eggs, which the male tree frog envelopes in milky sperm. The loose mass of eggs is snagged on small twigs or grasses.

47.

Wednesday 24 July 2020, 415.35 ppm.
Midday. Mowich campsite. Skyline II. Manning Park
Mosquitoes. Bees. Flies. Cicadas. Further off, grouse. Tum, tum, tum, tum, tum. Droning. Buzzing. This constant background hum. And all last night, an owl marking his territory, not far off.

Tuesday 4 August 2020, 412.86 ppm
Hot days for two, three weeks now. Wildfires in the Interior and on Vancouver Island sparked by lightning. And a massive wildfire out of control in California, the 'Apple Fire.' Parts of Australia back in COVID-19 lockdown, and it is ravaging

48. Each egg is roughly 1 millimetre in size.

49. The tadpoles look like black ink squiggles.

50. The tadpoles have been seen clustered together like a small black mirror to concentrate the sun. This speeds up metamorphosis.

51.

52. The tadpoles eat periphyton, filamentous algae, diatoms, pollen.

53. The tadpoles are eaten by almost everything: diving beetle larvae, bluegill sunfish, long-toed salamander larvae, dragon fly larvae, bullfrogs, garter snakes, jays.

54. This experiment will determine the relative presence in water, sediment, and whole frog tissue of more than 90 currently-used pesticides and pesticide degradates, using gas chromatography-mass spectrometry.

55. As tadpoles metamorphose, the eye lens flattens to accommodate light's speed in air.

---

some countries—the Philippines, the US—the border still closed with Canada. But this seems all at a distance. The parks and patios fill up every night. It is hard to find camp fuel, camping gear generally, as everyone is camping—MEC has been pillaged. It is almost impossible to buy a bike.

Friday 7 August 2020, 412.83 ppm. Evening. Illal Meadows
Hiked up from the Tulameen Forest Service Road yesterday through second growth forest, scree slope, stepped meadows, the wind growing as we climbed; then icy rain to the high meadow, where we set up the tent in a cleared site near a fire ring. Same mist and cold today—it pours down off the remaining licks of snow. The meadow is laced with clear, trickling streams. Patches of scree. White

56. They stop eating, as their mouths and digestive tracts are rearranged.

57. Within days on land, they absorb their tails.

58.

59. They leave no fossil record.

60. They have been recorded by web cams in eagle nests *atop trees so tall they scrape the fog for moisture…hopping about capturing insects.*

61. *Two fungicides, pyraclostrobin and tebuconazole, and one herbicide, simazine, were the most frequently detected pesticides in tissue samples.*

62. *It can be concluded that* H. regilla *has control over and can change its hue, chroma, and lightness during time periods on the order of minutes…*

63. P. regilla *is a habitat generalist that may be more resilient to habitat loss and fragmentation, and our results suggest they may not be especially vulnerable to more rapid drying rates expected in the future…*

---

heather. Pink heather. Alpine daisies. Flowers I can't name—white, blue, pink. Krummholz skirts the edges.

Climate crisis: Out-of-control wildfires in Arctic circle released more CO2 in two months than whole of 2019

Thursday 13 August 2020, 412.88 ppm

Late last night, a text from N. to share a Bill McKibben review of *Our Final Warning: Six Degrees of Climate Emergency.* Mark Lynas writes,

If we stay on the current business-as-usual trajectory, we could see two degrees as soon as the early 2030s, three degrees around mid-century, and four degrees by 2075 or so. If we're unlucky with

64. For a long time, I had forgotten them. But now I remember. I listen to their faint pulse every spring.

65.

66.

67. *Krrrrr-rk. Krik-ek.*

68. Systole. Diastole. Systole.

69. My love. My love. My love.

70. *Krik-eck.*

---

positive feedbacks….from thawing permafrost in the Arctic or collapsing tropical rainforests, then we could be in for five or even six degrees by century's end.

This morning, I scan the headlines. COVID flaring up in New Zealand, and again in Europe. World total infected approaching 21 million. Plagues of field mice in Germany. Another wildfire north of Los Angeles. Brazil has had 10 000 fires in August. Trump has rolled back methane climate standards for the American oil and gas industry. A sudden bee die-off in Italy, and when I search again to find the link, typing in 'bees,' 'dying,' 'Italy,' I find an article from 1st May 2020 that reads, *A viral disease that causes honey bees to suffer severe trembling, flightlessness, and death within a week is spreading exponentially in Britain.* First described by

17. SARS-CoV2

… a spectrum may exist between what is certainly alive and what is not. A rock is not alive … But what about a seed? A seed … has a potential for life, and it may be destroyed. In this regard, viruses resemble seeds more than they do live cells …. So life itself is an emergent, complex state, but it is made from the same fundamental, physical building blocks that constitute a virus … though not fully alive … they verge on life.

—Luis P. Villarreal, 2004

Between the first and second wave, which they'd warned will come by Fall, we hiked Hollyburn to Blue Gentian. First time in the forest after months of sheltering in place, surfacing through bluegreen tree light. Western hemlock, sword fern, pink twists of salmonberry; then buds and unfurled leaves as we climbed past rusted litter of needles; second growth and a skid road; back to an earlier season, before clearcuts, before the virus; to ancient cedars and snow. Trying to see again, all the little things, and what I can't see:

Aristotle, but this is a more virulent strain that might be caused by industrial bee keeping.

N. texts, i like very ancient texts as a kind of antidote to the present.

My daughter has decided to raise 3 chickens and is building a coop and chicken run in the backyard.

Saturday 22 August 2020, 412.52 ppm

The chicks are here, from a farm in Delta—'rainbow' clutch of 3 different varieties. They're gorgeous, 2 days old. The 2 largest look the same (perhaps they are the same kind), tea-coloured, with black beaks and streaks on their tiny wings; and one has gigantic eyes outlined in black, as if rimmed with kohl. These two are

called Stella and Ethel. The smallest one is called Dandelion; she's tawny and sunny coloured. She looks scrappy. They cuddle up next to a teddy bear in the brooder M. built, but come out to explore, to peck at their feed, to sip water. Stella likes to look at herself in the mirror.

Back from three days at Helm Creek in Garibaldi. The campsite was almost empty. Hiked w./ Y. across the cinder plane, under the shadow of Black Tusk— *T'ak't'ak mu'yin tl'ain7in'a'xe7en*—Landing Place of the Thunderbird. Crushed black volcanic rock—a paler line marking the trail. Chalk green of Helm Lake. Then up through stepped subalpine meadows to the base of the volcanic plug. Garibaldi Lake. Sphinx glacier. The Tantalus Range. Rain in the night, and again the day we left.

112

microscopic tardigrade, zooid, diatom, amoeba, alga, virion. This
organism at the edge of life, 50 nanometers in diameter—slip of RNA
and capsid that has slowed the world, slipped sideways from pangolin
to human or escaped from a virology lab in Wuhan.

Riboviria | Orthornavirae | Pisuviricota |
Pisoniviricetes | Nidovirales | Coronaviridae | Betacoronavirus | Sarbecovirus
| SARS-CoV-2, with an affinity to the *receptor angiotensin*
converting enzyme 2 (ACE2) on human cells. In the electron micrograph,
it looks like a child's crayon drawing of a flower or maybe a sea monster—
red violet circled by goldenrod and studded with little turquoise spikes.
There are ten million viruses in a teaspoon of seawater. Virions stream
around the earth, above the weather; all rain down 800 million
on every square metre, rain down RNA, rain DNA. O little virions.
O diatoms. O tardigrades. O mosses. O virion of the horizontal
gene transfer. Reservoir of genetic diversity. Driver of evolution.
O virion of the last universal common ancestor.

As we climbed, I touched
the knitted blanket of mosses grown on every ancient cedar along
the path's edge. I didn't have words to identify each kind, or even to know
if it was moss or liverwort. Each expressing a genetic language
in green structures. Gametophyte. Rhizoid. Feathered or slender.
Phyllids. Archegonia and antheridia. The filamentous seta of
sporophytes. Oregon leaf moss. Juniper haircap. Hoary rock. Pipe cleaner.

Three large wildfires in the Okanagan and the Kootenays. BC Wildfire
Service: *The #BCWildfire Service continues to respond to the Doctor Creek wild-*
fire (N21257) located 25 km SW of #CanalFlats. The fire is currently estimated to
be roughly 400 ha in size and is displaying aggressive fire behaviour.
The WHO announces we might not rein in the pandemic until the end of 2022.
And this is good news. 800 000 confirmed deaths reported today.

Thursday 3 September 2020, 411.72 ppm
Working on building the chicken coop. A string of hot days ahead. This article on
phys.org:

Sphagnum. Snow—suddenly, more snow as we ascended to
Blue Gentian; more and more, the lake still frozen, winter still.
But we cannot go back. We are an emergent, complex state;
evolving. Cro-Magnon sewing needles and antler-tipped spears.
Ochre and hematite drawings of the spirits of animals.
Smart phones and Gore-Tex and bicycles. Penicillin. CRISPR.
Our technologies. Our alphabets and poems. Our rituals. The stories
we tell of our future. We can interrupt the usual signals.
We can't go back. But we can go sideways. We can change.

*NEW MATHEMATICAL METHOD SHOWS HOW CLIMATE CHANGE
LED TO FALL OF ANCIENT CIVILIZATION:* Shifting monsoon patterns
led to the demise of the Indus Valley Civilization, a Bronze Age civiliza-
tion contemporary to Mesopotamia and ancient Egypt.
The climate emergency action committee was voted 90% in favour of at the union
AGM. Now I am drawing up a draft of the terms of reference, and a call out for
committee members. Things move so slowly. *This is an emergency.* We need to
respond as we have to COVID.

18.)⋅⋅#⋅+⟨

ogam
(The Tree Alphabet)

It hé a n-airde: desdruim, túathdruim, lesdruim, tredruim, imdruim. Is amlaid im-drengar Ogum amal im-drengar crann .i. saltrad fora frém in chroinn ar tús 7 do lám dess remut 7 do lám clé fo déoid. Is íarsin is leis 7 is fris 7 is trít 7 is immi. Their orientations are: right of the stemline, left of the stemline, across the stemline, through the stemline, around the stemline. Ogam is climbed (i.e. read) as a tree is climbed, i.e. treading on the root of the tree first with one's right hand before one and one's left hand last. After that it is across it and against it and through it and around it.

> —from the *Auraicept na n-Éces*, The Poet's Primer, translation by Damian McManus

---

Tuesday 8 September, -- ppm (data too variable). 6am

Days of 31 degrees but bluedark, cool mornings. Wildfires growing in California. J35, Tahlequah, has given birth to a new calf—J57. She's the one who carried her dead calf on her back for 17 days several years ago, as if in mourning.

We have had comprehensive encounters with J pod in Haro Strait on September 1 and 3, 2020, at which times we monitored pregnant females J35 and J41 very carefully and saw that they had not yet given birth. On September 5, we followed up on a report from one of the PWWA whale watchers that a very small calf was seen. Our researchers, Dave Ellifrit and Katie Jones, accompanied by guest veterinarian Dr. Sarah Bahan, quickly identified the

т beith   Young paper birch in Malcolm Knapp, trunk like burnished copper.

╥ luis   Fir bonsai in the shadow of Black Tusk,
          t'ak't'ak mo'yin tl'a in7in'a'xe7en.

╥╥ fearn   Red alder flickers silver/green in the wind.

╥╥╥ sail   *Salix Babylonica, Salix lucinda,* I wept, I wept.

╥╥╥╥ nion   Pitch of Sitka spruce on the Juan de Fuca trail.

⊥ uath   Scoured krumholz in Illal Meadows,
          Cupressus nootkakensis.

⊥⊥ dair   The Garry oak meadow at Drumbeg, the camas lillies, the crickets.

⊥⊥⊥ tinne   Arbutus peels smooth to salmon.

⊥⊥⊥⊥ coll   Beaked hazelnut sprouts after fire.

⊥⊥⊥⊥⊥ ceirt   Little green fruits of Pacific crabapple.

ɟ muin   Trailing blackberry, *Rubus ursinus,* purple scat of bear.

ɟɟ gor   A trail of ink-smudged salal along the beach at Ruckle.

ɟɟɟ nGéadal   Western swordfern, everywhere, everywhere.

ɟɟɟɟ straif   And the dusky pink of Nootka rose.

ɟɟɟɟɟ ruis   Red elderberry along the Tulameen Forest Service Road.

– ailm   Columns of lodgepole pine in the bog hold up the sky.

–– onn   Western red cedar, *Thuja plicata, xepá:y*—the one who is carved.

––– ur   White rhododendron below Illal, cupfuls of bees.

–––– eadhadh   Black cottonwood in the Okanagan, handfuls of cotton and wildfire ash.

––––– iodhadh   Pacific yew, its cone like a tiny red berry, that clasps only one seed.

---

mother as J35, Tahlequah. She made world news in the summer of 2018 when she carried her dead calf on her head for 17 days while the pod traveled about 1,000 miles around the Salish Sea on what we termed a "Tour of Grief." She was still capable of producing a live calf after an approximate eighteen-month gestation! Hooray! Her new calf appeared healthy and precocious, swimming vigorously alongside its mother in its second day of free-swimming life. We know that it was not born today because its dorsal fin was upright, and we know that it takes a day or two to straighten after being bent over in the womb, so we assign its birthday as September 4, 2020. (Ergo gestation commenced in February 2019). Tahlequah was mostly separate from the other whales and

19. GAIA
(biosphere, the carnal field)

This intertwined web of experience is, of course, the 'life-world' to which Husserl alluded in his final writings, yet now the life-world has been disclosed as a profoundly carnal field, as this very dimension of smells and tastes and chirping rhythms warmed by the sun and shivering with seeds. It is, indeed, nothing other than the biosphere— the matrix of earthly life in which we ourselves are embedded.
[ ]
My body is a sort of open circuit that completes itself only in things, in others, in the encompassing earth...
      —David Abram, *The Spell of the Sensuous*

A. sends me a screenshot of *Elysia* in response to my poem—
So beautiful an ornament to this world and most likely will move
to another soon, an underworld...Robert Macfarlane mentions
the Saami belief that the dead live in an underworld that mirrors
our own...Could our mirror world be populated by extinct creatures?

---

being very evasive as she crossed the border into Canada, so we ended our encounter with her after a few minutes and wished them well on their way.
–Center for Whale Research

Wednesday 9 September 2022, 411.26 ppm
There was a sweet burning smell yesterday that grew and grew, and a haze in the air. My sister texted to say it was smoke from the forest fires in Washington State, drifting north. The Institute for Economics and Peace says 1.2 billion people in 31 countries may be displaced by ecological threats by 2050. They've begun a new ecological threat register. "Lack of resilience will lead to worsening food insecurity and competition over resources, increasing civil unrest and mass displacement."

Yes, I think of how many have gone through. The *Elysia* unfurls
its wings. Emerald chloroplasts stitch sunlight to carbon. In the salt
marshes of Texas. The blue crabs. The mud crabs. Stitch calcium.
Form chitin. Chilean tarweed and sea kale. Sea angel. Sea salp.
The chaotic nanostructure of *espejitos*, little mirrors tangle the light.
Sea kelp. Salal. Stitch carbon to hydrogen. The assembly of
light-gathering machinery. Paper birch. Nootka rose. Western sword fern.
Capture light in narrow wave-length windows. Salmonberry.
Thimbleberry. Release oxygen. The rare bright elements; the soft,
the clear, the blue. Hydrogen joins helium. The fusion ash of stars
seeded through the universe. Calcium. Cobalt. Copper. Carbon.
Stitch carbon to hydrogen. Release oxygen. Dandelions.

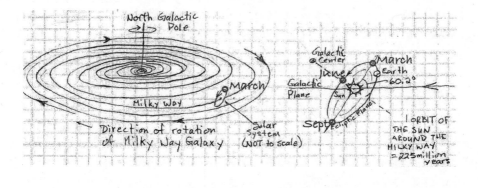

Thursday 10 September 2020, 411.0 ppm
Wildfires burning across Washington State, Oregon, California. San Francisco
looks like a scene out of *Bladerunner.*

> Climate scientists blame global warming for extreme wet and dry seasons in the
> US West that have caused grasses and scrub to flourish then dry out, leaving
> abundant fuel for fires. 'We do not have a context for this amount of fire in
> the landscape,' said Oregon's chief of Fire Protection, 'seeing them run down
> the canyons the way they have—carrying tens of miles in an afternoon and not
> slowing down in the evening—there's absolutely no context for that in this en-
> vironment.' (Al Jazeera).

Meadowrue. The honey bee. The bumble bee. Sip nectar.
Gather pollen. Spiracles of oxygen. Sweet burn and hover.
Western pasqueflower. Yellow glacier lily. Heathers. Sunlight. Carbon.
The engineers. Make honeypots. Make paper cells. The obscure yellow
pigment *xanthopterin* of *Vespa orientalis*. Harvest solar energy. Dig nests.
Dig lily bulbs. Fix nitrates in subalpine meadows. Remember the hum of bees
in white rhododendrons at Illal. See this tiny snail, *Angostopila Dominika*
in the limestone cliffs of Guangxi, China? See how it fits in the eye of
a sewing needle. Take notes—*Carbon (C) is a non-metal which easily links
to itself and other elements. Life is dependent upon the chemical qualities
of carbon.* Gaia is *an emergent property of interactions among organisms.*
Our neuron cells include the basket, the cartwheel, the chandelier, starburst,
spindle, pyramidal, stellate, granule, and double bouquet.
A "back of the envelope calculation" in 1972 estimated that our microbiome
outnumbers our own cells by ten to one. This assembly of light-gathering
machinery. Luca, our last universal common ancestor: root
of the tree of life, rooted in metallic darkness. Noctiluca. Sitka
spruce. Dark-eyed junco. Remember the soot-coloured moth at Semaphore
alighting on the page. Write, *Cobalt (Co) is a rare, bright, whitish-blue metal,*
magnetic, needed for root function. Write, blue thinks itself within me,
*I surrender a part of my body, even my whole body, to this particular moment
of vibrating and filling space known as blue*…Blue gentian, penstemon,

---

Friday 11 September 2020, -- ppm (data too variable)
Woke up again to the sweet scent of burning. Forest fires out of control on the
west coast. Hazy blue sky. Half a million being evacuated from Portland.

Saturday 12 September 2020, 411.24 ppm
I can tell the smoke is here the moment I open my eyes because the light is differ-
ent—even behind closed lids—dim, orange, diffuse. No direct rays of sunlight. No
shadows. Like waking on an alien planet.
>   Authorities said more than 1500 sq miles have burned in Oregon in
>   recent days, newly double the number in a typical year. Hundreds of

stickseed, the blue-eyed grass. The light reactions. Remember the night before
we climbed Desolation? We stood on the dark shore at Lightning Creek.
We stood on the earth, on the Orion arm. We stood in time,
looking into the galactic centre, looking into ourselves—these temporary
sentient forms, bodies of fusion ash and starlight.

---

firefighters are battling 2 large blazes that threatened to merge near
the most populated part of the state, including suburbs of Portland.
If the fires merge, they could generate enough heat to send embers
thousands of feet into the air, potentially igniting other areas. — *The
Guardian* 12 Sept 2020

Monday 14 September 2020, 411.68 ppm
Woke up to foghorns. It's been cooler the last few days. There's colour at sunrise,
but otherwise the sky is grey like a haze of cigarette smoke. The entire west coast
of the US is burning.

20. ᴛ, *k'i,*
Betula

ᴛ, *beith*, birch, first letter of ogam 〉⊸#+〈 the tree language.

Is there something it is like to be a birch tree, in the conversion of sunlight to
green shadows and tree flesh?

We had not seen each other for weeks, except by Skype. We walked the river
trails along the Saskatchewan.

The word "birch," qwəłin, *is present in ancient Proto-Salish … indicative of
its use at the base of the language.*

qwəłin, qw əł?in-az', qw łínłp, qw qw łin', sə kw 'əmiy, haawak̲' , k'i, k'ih,
k'ii ◁·ᴬᖯ·ᐟ ᒥᗄᴬ, wigwaas, silver birch, canoe birch, Kenai birch,
paper birch.

*The word for "birch" is also very ancient in the Athabaskan language, an
unanalyzable monosyllable that reconstructs back to at least the Proto-
Athabaskan language, and perhaps dates to an even earlier language stock:
Proto-Athabaskan-Eyak-Tlingit.*

Wednesday 16 September 2020, -- ppm (data too variable)
No change. Diffused grey light and the sun a small disc, tinted pink. Ashen Loopen
moths everywhere—like shreds of burnt paper from a fire.

> Fire itself is sacred. It renews life. It shades rivers and cools the water's tem-
> perature. It clears brush and makes for sufficient food for large animals. It
> changes the molecular structure of traditional food and fiber resources making
> them nutrient dense and more pliable. Fire does so much more than western
> science currently understands.
> —*The Guardian*, Bill Tripp., 16 Sept 2020

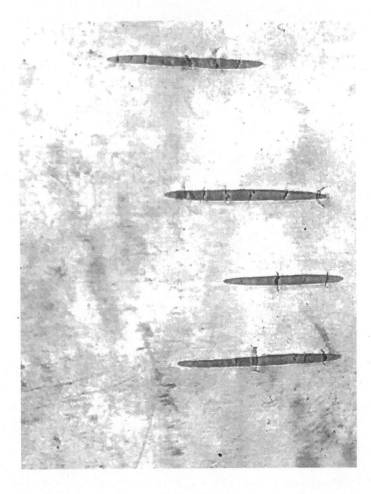

Friday 18 September 2020, 411.18 ppm
One of my students wrote in a discussion forum yesterday, "It feels like the world is ending." I'd asked them to watch *Before the Flood*, and to read a textbook on climate change. A podcast yesterday had an expert who predicted the fire season in California will be year-round. The Pantanal Wetlands in the Amazon are on fire—it never burns. A fire larger than the fires in California. It is the 11th day now of this oppressive smoke. The sun melts a tiny pink hole in the sky, like a cigarette burn. No shadows. The second COVID wave has begun. Yet another report that SARS-Cov-2 is a chimera, constructed on the backbone of the Zooshan ZC45 and ZXC21 strains.

In the sunlight, which sluices down. Stitch carbon to carbon.

Leaves, leaves. A lung. An eye. Eyes. Dilating to sun.

To remove a bark strip from the tree, two cuts were made horizontally and
one vertically with a sharpened tool, and the bark piece was peeled off in a
rectangular sheet …

Light. Dark. Light. Dark. Light.

Some of the earliest Buddhist manuscripts are written in black ink on
strips of birch bark. The Kharoṣṭhī manuscripts, circa first century
common era, were preserved in clay jars: a Dharmapada, avadānas,
Purvayogas, Abhidharma, Khargaviṣaṇa-sutra, or Rhinoceros sutra—

endure troubles
wander alone
like the rhinoceros

The scrolls were reinforced by a thread sewn along both margins. In a few cases,
traces of the original thread are preserved and in many places, the needle
holes along the margins are still visible.

It was along the banks of the Saskatchewan. The city veiled in smoke
from BC wildfires. I could taste the ash on my tongue.

VIROLOGIST RELEASES PAPER CLAIMING CORONAVIRUS MADE IN CHINESE LAB
By Keoni Everington, *Taiwan News*, Staff Writer
2020/09/15 17:13 TAIPEI (Taiwan News)—A Chinese virologist and
whistleblower on Monday (Sept. 14) followed through on her pledge to
release a paper explaining how the genome of the Wuhan coronavirus
(COVID-19) indicates that it was constructed in a Chinese lab rather
than naturally occurring.
　　For the past few months, Yan Li-Meng (閻麗夢), a virologist em-
ployed as a researcher at the University of Hong Kong's School of

I saw lenticels for the first time. Stitches in pale bark, a thin gash stitched
closed.

Is there something it is like to breathe oxygen in through so many gaping
mouths in skin? o o o

The Bakhshali manuscript from the second century common era consists
of mathematical formulae and rules drawn on fragments of birch
bark—rules for algorithms, quadratic equations, negative numbers
and so on are written in verse, followed by prose elaboration. It
includes the earliest known use of a symbol for zero, to become the
shunya-bindu, 'dot of the empty place.'

	or			or		or							
1		2			3		4	5	6	7	8	9	0

Zero, *the seed of an idea.*

Sips of oxygen.

We were breathing in the ash of trees. It was as if the air were filled with a
fine-crushed chalk. And it was very still.

Public Health when the coronavirus pandemic began, has been al-
leging that the coronavirus came from a Chinese lab and that it is a
chimera based on the "Zhoushan bat coronavirus." According to Yan,
an examination of the genome sequences released by the Chinese
government on Jan. 14 also shows that the Zhoushan ZC45 and
ZXC21 strains are the closest to SARS-CoV-2 and that they are the
"backbone" upon which COVID-19 was constructed.

Monday 28 September 2020, 410.67 ppm
Another baby orca was born on Friday, to mother J41, near Sheringam, BC. And

It can be so hard to speak after a long absence. The body needs to acclimate.
We wandered the shore trails, alternating silence and faltering talk,
like a Super 8 film—image and sound out of synch.

And the sun? How does it feel to need the sun in this way, green
    wavelengths reflected, its warmth absorbed by a multitude of
    trembling leaves?

There is another way to describe this, in the language of elements:

$$6CO2 + 6H_2O \xrightarrow{\text{light}} C_6H_{12}O_6 + 6\,O2$$

The Bower manuscript of the 6th century common era, found near
    Kuchar along the old Silk Road north of Takla Makan, transcribes a
    recipe for soma, inscribed on birch bark:

Fig. 1. Pôthi of the Bower Manuscript, taken from Hoernle (2011, Plate VII).

---

the calf born to Tahlequah is doing OK so far. "Now is the time for the region to
work to make sure there is enough chinook for the southern residents, including
the lactating and expecting mothers…It is not just the total number of chinook
that matter. The whales need big chinook. The fish also need to be in the orcas'
feeding range, where they have learned through generations uncounted to suc-
cessfully target chinook." *phys.org*

Wednesday 30 September 2020, 410.87 ppm
Kew has released its annual *State of the World's Plants and Fungi* report. 40%
of the world's plants threatened with extinction. Mostly it focusses on the uses

And when the whole is reduced to one-eighth of the original quantity, boil in it pastes made of fine powder of one pala each of the following drugs: Balâ, Nâgabalâ, Jîvâ, cowhage, Nata, juice of sugar-cane, Sprikkà, small cardamoms and cinnamon-bark, Jîvaka, Rishabhaka, Mêdâ, Madhuka, and blue lotus, the colour producing saffron, aloe-wood, and cinnamon-leaves, Vidârî, Kshîrakakôlî, Vîrâ, and Śârivâ, Śatâvarî, Priyangu, Gudûchî, filaments of the lotus, Lâmajjaka, red and white sandal, and fruits of Râjâdana, pearl, coral, conch-shell, moon-stone, sapphire, crystal, silver, gold, and other gems and pearls, liquorice, madder, and Am□umatî. Boil the whole slowly over a gentle fire with four pâtra of (sweet) oil and eight times as much of milk, adding also tamarind juice and vinegar of rice, one half as much as the milk. This boiling should be repeated a hundred or even a thousand times; and when it is thoroughly done, it may be known by this sign, that on the approach of the proper time the oil stiffens by exposure to the rays of the sun.

Lenticular mouths opening to darkness.

I have read that consciousness might be understood as intrinsic to matter—part of every cell, like chromosomes. That at a certain threshold, with a certain mass of cells, there is emergence of a consciousness that we might recognize as human. But that even consciousness can be thought of as a continuum, like a faint background hum in the world that sometimes breaks through as bird song or nigun.

---

of plants for humans: "humans rely on just 15 plants to serve 90% of our food needs, adding to the problem of malnutrition and leaving us vulnerable to climate change, but scientists at Kew have identified 7,039 plant species that could be used as food." CNN. Robin Wall Kimmerer writes, we should first be asking ourselves, what do we have to give?

Tuesday 6 October 2020, 411.23 ppm
The north shore is hazy again with smoke from the wildfires. There's a new word to describe the August complex fire in North California—*gigafire,* a fire larger than 1 million acres. Tawahum Bige, who was one of the poets I met at Art Song 2020, was sentenced to 28 days in jail this morning for participating in a ceremony in

Light. Dark. Light.

We try to speak across a gulf as wide as the universe.

How does paper birch experience the qualia of deep blue or ash,
    the cut of a knife?

There were curls of birch bark wide enough to clasp my wrist, littered here
    and there. It wasn't clear which had sloughed off naturally and which
    had been peeled.

Wigwaasabak, birch bark scrolls, were used by the Ojibway/Anishinaabe
    people to inscribe maps and geometrical patterns. Mide-wiigwaas
    of the Midewiwin, the Grand Medicine Society, recorded sacred
    knowledge of the Mide.

Sacred Ojibwa scrolls found after 70 years
CBC News · Posted: May 09, 2000 8:50 AM ET |
Last Updated: May 9, 2000

In the 1930s, an American anthropologist named Irving Hallowell
journeyed north to Canada to live among the Ojibwa and study
their culture. He left with a wealth of knowledge—and something
else. He took a bundle of sacred scrolls, made out of birch bark,
and central to the performance of ancient religious ceremonies
of the tribe. The scrolls were never forgotten by those whose
ancestors used them. Some elders in the tribe remember the

---

protest of the Transmountain pipeline. I know because they posted an update to
Instagram. I have been teaching on Zoom all day. M. has a blackeye and a cut
finger from working on the chicken coop. We had the first meeting of the climate
committee at the college. The leaves are turning colour: crimson, gold.

Monday 12 October 2020, 411.10 ppm
    Fifth of countries at risk of ecosystem collapse, analysis finds
    Trillions of dollars of GDP depend on biodiversity, according to Swiss
    Re report
    One-fifth of the world's countries are at risk of their ecosystems
    collapsing because of the destruction of wildlife and their habitats,

old ways of doing things. Elder Donald Bird still uses the sweat lodge behind his house. There were other rituals, like the drum and the shaking tent, used to conjure the souls of the living and the dead.

Friday, 8 November 2019. New Westminster, at the college. Feast With A Poet at the Aboriginal Gathering Place. A talk by Liz Howard on her poetic practice, a projected image of a birch bark scroll, overhead, from a book written by an uncle.

I have also read that consciousness is simply the hallucination of a lived body. Or is it epiphenomenal, just as smoke drifts from a fire. But there is still this lived feeling—what it is like to be. I trust this intuition.

Crystalline needles thread bark. Layers of botulin.

There was often the same delay by Skype, words not quite matched to lips, a lag between question and response. Or the image would freeze and go dark, the connection lost.

$C30H50O2$. Betulin. Betuline. Whitening.

Birch bark postcard, from the Gulag, Inventory No. TR424. Written by *political prisoner Antanos Baniulis (1892-1945) to his daughter, Dana*

---

according to an analysis by the insurance firm Swiss Re. Natural "services" such as food, clean water and air, and flood protection have already been damaged by human activity. More than half of global GDP—$42tn (£32tn)—depends on high-functioning biodiversity, according to the report, but the risk of tipping points is growing. Countries including Australia, Israel and South Africa rank near the top of Swiss Re's index of risk to biodiversity and ecosystem services, with India, Spain and Belgium also highlighted. Countries with fragile ecosystems and large farming sectors, such as Pakistan and Nigeria, are also flagged up.
    —*The Guardian*, 12 October 2020

Baniulytė (born 1924), who was in exile in the settlement Kazachii, Ust'-Iansk Region of the Yakutsk ASSR. The stamp of the military censor is on the envelope, and there are sections that have been deleted by the censor.

Springwood, latewood. Springwood, latewood.

INSPECTED
BY MILITARY CENSOR
KRASNOYARSK
123/128

1943 ¹⁸/₅

My Dear Ones,
I have received one letter from you.
had no
Petkevichi we ~~but no~~ were lucky
to another place ▬▬▬
▬▬▬▬▬▬▬▬▬▬
▬▬▬▬▬ The one who gets parcels
has a good life, he can have
tobacco or work. In exchange for tobacco
I will [illegible] to survive. I think that for you
it is of no importance. Write what work
you are working at.   A. Baniulis

Reddened buds at branch tips, ripen to catkin.

Sunday 18 October 2020, 411.17 ppm
Early. Overcast. At Y.'s. Hiked up to Elfin Lakes Friday, surprised by the snow as we crossed over into the subalpine. Someone had used a shovel to clear a tent platform. We were the only ones, and a single dark quail along the path. We stopped and looked at each other a long minute before it flew off.

Thursday 22 October 2020, 412.05 ppm
For the first time since records began, the main nursery of Arctic sea ice in Siberia has yet to start freezing in late October. Could have impacts across the Arctic. Ocean temperatures there 5 degrees Celsius above average. Graphs of sea-ice

The voids that mar Gulag correspondences are as evocative of the conditions that produced them as their messages. Occasional black marks left by censors; pages torn or rendered illegible as the result of water damage; everything that inmates and their relations do not say...

Some of the birch trees had been cut with the initials of letters. On one trunk, a rectangle of bark had been removed with surgical precision. Peels of greyish-white bark littered the ground like bandages.

956 catalogued *gramoty*—texts, letters—written on *beresty*, strips of birch bark, were discovered in Novgorod during Soviet times. These dated from the medieval period.

Gramoty fragment No.827. Mid-12th century. Drawing of two interlocking birds. The words:

ОУАМЫШЬЛИШ[Ь]ЛИЖЄ

and we went on and on

Dust of ochre pollen. Thin scratching chickadees. Sapsucker, *tap tap*.

Gramoty fragment No.521. Early 15th century. Catalogued as a love spell.

---

extent in the Laptev Sea, which usually show a healthy seasonal pulse, appear to have flat-lined.
  — The Guardian.

Saturday 31 October 2020, 412.27 ppm. Halloween. Blue moon. 11:12pm
Fireworks at the park. Biked to the Museum of Anthropology at the university this afternoon. Brisk, sunny day. Hiked down to Tower Beach to read. Studied chloroplasts, the nature of pigment and how a green pigment captures and translates sunlight from the visible spectrum into chemical energy, sugar molecules. Chloroplasts move in response to sunlight—stacking themselves in columns or aligning themselves edgewise to reduce exposure. And wondered, can we use

----такъсʌрозго
рисртцетвоѥите
ло(т)[в]оѥидшʌтвоʌ
доменеидотеладомо
ѥгоидовидудомоѥго

---*so let your heart*
and body be kindled
and your soul for me
and for my body
and for my face

A tightening. Little shivers. Sap flow.

Gramoty fragment No.199, 203. 13th century. Several drawings of mystical beings and warriors, attributed to a little boy called Onfim, practicing his letters.

---

the idea of photosynthesis to create renewable energy? Or can humans learn to photosynthesize? Imagine if we could live like trees.

Monday 2 November 2020, 411.55 ppm. All Souls
A storm is coming from the Pacific, to hit overnight. But this morning there is sunlight. Ochre leaves. A few stray cosmos.

Monday 9 November 2020, 412.23 ppm
Still dark. More COVID restrictions as cases climb exponentially. But some bright spots—Biden/Harris confirmed as winners of the US election, which means at least a chance for a Green New Deal, and certainly a return to the Paris Accord. Maybe

ѦЗВѢРЬ

I am a beast

Late afternoon. The sun was a smoked pink disc. Everything softened by smoke, like a faded postcard. We followed the trail east as it wound along the river and led us to the footpath beneath the bridge.

Carbon to carbon to carbon. Hydrogen. Oxygen.

Paper birch is often the first tree to grow in ravaged areas. It can take root in the thinnest of soils, in sites disturbed by wildfire, avalanche, mine spoils—coal, lignite, rock phosphate, slate, oil-shale, bauxite, gold.

---

cancellation of the Keystone XL. And news this morning of an mRNA vaccine by Pfizer said to be 90% effective in clinical trials—but the sample is miniscule. They are already talking of producing 1.27 billion vaccines in 2021. It requires an ultra-cold supply chain of minus 80 °C. This will be difficult for all but the richest countries.

Thursday 19 November 2020, 412.44 ppm
ANTARCTICA'S BLUE WHALES RETURN TO SOUTH GEORGIA A CENTURY AFTER THEY WERE NEARLY WIPED OUT
The near-extinction of blue whales around South Georgia in the early 20th century may have resulted in the loss of their "cultural memory"

In undisturbed stands, it can make between 2.2 and 294 million seeds per acre. Its little, winged seeds dispersed by wind.

Springwood, latewood. Heartwood. Heartwood. Thickening.

It moves slowly. But for a tree, so fast. A birch tree lives only 150 years. It burns through life.

An itch. Tearing. Slow peel to pink salmon flesh.

A source of food for wintering moose. For white-tailed deer and snowshoe hares who feed on saplings. Porcupines on the inner bark. Ruffled grouse on the catkins and buds.

Green alder, beaked hazel, blackberry, raspberry, elder, gooseberry. Nearby.

Yellow-bellied sapsuckers drill holes in the bark. Hummingbirds and red squirrels feed at the sapwells.

A flight of winged seeds. Here, on this scorched ground.

Its leaves devoured by the bronze birch borer, tent caterpillar, birch skeletonizer, birch leafminer, the saddled prominent, the gypsy moth, the sparmarked black moth, sawflies, cambium miners.

---

of the abundance there of Antarctic krill—tiny swimming crustaceans found in huge swarms in the Southern Ocean and the only food of blue whales. Knowledge of whale feeding grounds may be passed on from mother whales to their calves. "There was a cultural memory, maybe, of animals that used to come to South Georgia that was lost because they were wiped out," Calderan said. "They couldn't pass on the knowledge of the feeding grounds because there weren't any of them left." But the evidence of the recent survey suggested at least some blue whales have rediscovered South Georgia's abundance of krill.

Embryonic roots split the seed coat. Take hold in thin mineral soil.

Microorganisms enter the wounds. *Inonotus obliqua. Phellinus igniarius. Nectria galligena.*

A shoot, through mineral waste. A clearing. Blue.

We stepped into the metal underpass and walked out over the river. You said the birch tree refugia marked an earlier migration, trees that remained as the ice retreated north.

Sunlight. A leaf and a leaf. Stitch carbon to water. Leaves.

Leaves greening. Carbon to carbon. Lignin. Heartwood. The sapwood runs.

You told me of birchbark canoes, lightweight and waterproof. That birch burns very hot.

I have since learned the common word for 'birch' in Indo-European is a verb, *to shine.*

Yellow birch, grey birch. Kin.

Friday 20 November 2020, 412.38 ppm
An Indigenous consortium—4 First Nations in Alberta, 1 in Saskatchewan—are investing a billion dollars in the KeystoneXL, "designed to transport up to 830,000 barrels per day of oil from Alberta to Nebraska." It is said this will convince Biden to approve the project. Extinction Rebellion blocked a rail line on Tuesday along the route of the Transmountain pipeline expansion route, at North Road and the Trans-Canada highway.
More lockdown restrictions here.
More rain. Less hope.

To make a birch bark container: *Women would stitch together the edge seams with a bone awl and split roots of spruce, Western redcedar, or cottonwood, and then caulk the seams with pitch.*

We can't even identify the neural correlates of consciousness in humans.

Dense cakes of dehydrated berries, cherries, and rosehips were boiled with hot stones in birch bark and cedar root baskets.

Where might the correlates be in trees?

Pin cherry, red maple, Jack pine or ash. Nearby.

Saponin from the leaves, crushed as soap. Resin as waterproof glue. A Firestarter. A light canoe. Bread from the inner bark ground up as flour. Sap fresh or fermented as wine.

Of Birch-Wine. As well in thefe Northern parts of *Europe*, as in many places of *Afia*, and *Africa*, may we extract the Blood of Trees themfelves, and make them drinkable. The delicacy of our Liquors made of Fruits and Grains, very much abates the eager profecution of fuch defigns, yet the pleafantnefs and falubrity of the Blood of feveral Trees, have given encouragement, to fome *Virtuofi*, to beftow their labour and skill on them, and not in vain, The *Sycomore* and *Wallnut*-Trees are faid to yield excellent Juice, but we in *England* have not had fo

---

Saturday 19 December 2020, 414.35 ppm
Rain all week. Another vaccine approved. First shots delivered. Slow roll out— perhaps everyone in Canada vaccinated by September 2021. A new strain that spreads more quickly detected in the UK. Climate committee—working on a sustainability microcredential, the speaker series to debut the first week of March. Strategizing with the union over how to get the college to declare a climate emergency and sign the SDGaccord. I'm drafting a motion to ask DCFA to do the same. And I've joined a student research committee so we can hire a student researcher to work on the sustainability hub, maybe create a poster and video for the speaker series and do a literature review on rewilding to present to the college. I've also

A 2000-year-old birch basket found at the Ollie site on the Canadian Plateau, ancestral land of the Tsilhqot'in, Dakelh, Secwepemc, and Upper Nlaka'pomux, contained seeds of Saskatoon and raspberry, tiny fragments of charcoal, blades of grass, salmonid bones.

Roots in darkness. Plaits mycelium. Sends signals, sugars. Links to kind.

Phytochemists are conducting ongoing studies to identify, extract, and test natural chemicals (pentacyclic triterpenes) present in birch bark for their antiallergic, anti-viral, anti-microbial, anti-malarial, hepatoprotective, anti-cancer, and anti-inflammatory effects.

Fomitopsis betulina, the birch bracket, filters out heavy metals like radio-caesium. An edible fungus with a distinct scent of green apples.

Carbon to carbon.

We walked out part way over the river, and then turned back. Taste of ash. Now talk, now silence.

Crackling of root tips in underground channels. Signals inaudible to humans.

Still this space between us. Maybe it is always there. Even when you know what I will say before I say it.

---

made some contacts with the DSU and we now have 2 students on board—one is the rep. for the implementation of campaigns and events, and one is the Indigenous students' rep. The hardest part is actually hearing back from other faculty on the committee—they say they want to join but don't come to meetings, don't communicate at all. But some people are amazing. Think of the Institution as analogous to the country, a heavy, slow-moving monolith dogged by its own plodding momentum—while there's utter inertia on board—about to slam into an iceberg. We need grassroots movement as catalyst. This winter break, I must draft a motion for the union to declare an emergency and sign the accord. And figure out how to create and circulate a petition, so the college will do the same.

Root tips reaching out to fungal threads, through dark soil.

A sentinel.

Scent of green apples. Of wintergreen.

I could taste it. The pall of trees in my lungs.

A redacted text, a postcard.

What little diffused light came through.

And then cold, cold. Stillness. Snow falls.

I drew a curl of birch bark around my wrist.

A lover's spell.

Shattered fruits. Glitter of seeds.

Ringed heartwood to record Siberian winters.

Genetic script unfurling.

Monday 21 December 2020, 414.50 ppm. 7:30pm. Winter Solstice
A winter storm—rain.
The longest night.
From here, there will be two more minutes of light each day.

Lenticels opening to take small breaths.

Soft pink. Ash.

Springwood, latewood. Springwood, latewood.

A refugee migrating north.

The pall of smoke.

Stitching the snow.

A memory of ice.

An alphabet.

A girl. A tree.

Beautiful cell.

Т, *k'i.*

Winged seed.

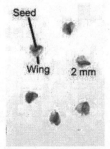

Notes

I. Wildfire

Manna
Descriptions of "manna" from "Manna", *Wikipedia*.

Ora
Come bride ... Yehuda Amichai, from *Travels*. Translated by Ruth Nevo.

Boreal
Human existence is so fragile a thing.... Simone Weil. *Gravity and Grace.*
Our 'on and off' reception of the world and *Rests and silences* ... Susan Stewart,
The Poet's Freedom: A Notebook. on Making.

Blackmud
The *Kol Dodi,* Voice of the Beloved, is drawn from the Song of Songs
2:8. Translation here is a conflation of several versions, primarily the King
James Version.

Whitemud
Psalm 147:3.

Iridium
*The earth has tilted on its axis. Qapirangajuq: Inuit Knowledge and Climate
Change.* Dir. Zacharias Kunuk.

Widgeon
*An I, an emotion, an ethos...*Mutlu Konuk Blasing. *Lyric Poetry: The Pain
and Pleasure of Words.*

Desolation

There are feral possibilities in the cities…and *In our hearts we all know the world will not be saved,* from *Desert,* Anon.

Ecocide demands a response… Paul Kingsnorth and Dougald Hine, *The Dark Mountain Manifesto.*

Paper birch

Tzama Lecha Nafshi, my soul thirsts for you. A niggun whose tune was popularized by the last Lubavitcher Rebbe. Words derived from Psalm 63: 2-3.

II. Seeds

This sequence thinks about forms of resistance, survival, and emergence in the context of climate change and the sixth mass extinction. Each numbered section or 'seed' centres on a different organism or human-made object: lentil, snowdrop, salmon, codex, chloroplast, tardigrade, the order *Hymenoptera,* tiny house, among others. The *Vespa orientalis,* as noted by Robert Bringhurst in *Learning to Die,* has evolved a band of the obscure pigment Xanthopterin to draw sunlight out of air and generate a small voltage. Pacific salmon travel thousands of miles to their spawning grounds in the Fraser River and feed the rich coastal ecosystem. The tiny houses, wood frame cabins outfitted with solar panels, are being built by the Tiny House Warriors in unceded Secwépemc Territory in the interior of BC to challenge the construction of the Trans Mountain pipeline. "Seeds" is inspired in part by *The Ecologist's* 1972 report, *A Blueprint for Survival,* which was warning almost half a century ago of species loss, pollutants, population demands on food and water, the harmful effects of industrial-scale agriculture, and the global economy's dangerous reliance on fossil fuels. I think of each 'seed' in this long poem as a blueprint, whether simple human-made tool or complex organism driven by its DNA to adapt to and respond to our current existential threat. I'm also interested in the idea of attention as a moral act, as observed by the neuroscientist Iain McGilchrist: "without alertness, we are as if asleep, unresponsive to the world around us; without vigilance, we cannot become aware of anything we do not already know." I want to focus attention as a form of respect for these organisms—not as resources, but as beings in their own right; withdrawn, dark noumena.

Epigraphs:
Definition of "serotiny," *Wiktionary*; *A Blueprint for Survival*, 1972; Muriel Rukeyser, *10th Elegy*.

I. τ *Shelter*
Italicized quote from Jack Kerouac, *Desolation Angels*.

2. π *Codex*
James Lovelock:

> One thing we can do to lessen the consequences of catastrophe is to write a guidebook for our survivors to help them rebuild civilization without repeating too many of our mistakes....an accurate record of all we know about the present and the past environment...a book of knowledge written so well as to constitute literature in its own right. Something for anyone interested in the state of the Earth and of us—a manual for living well and for survival. The quality of its writing must be such that it would serve for pleasure, for devotional reading, as a source of facts and even as a primary school text. It would range from simple things such as how to light a fire, to our place in the solar system and the universe. It would be a primer of philosophy and science—it would provide a top-down look at the Earth and us. It would explain the natural selection of all living things, and give the key facts of medicine, including the circulation of the blood, the role of the organs … It would explain properties like temperature, the meaning of their scales of measurement and how to measure them. It would list the periodic table of the elements. It would give an account of the air, the rocks, and the oceans …
> It would also be the survival manual for our successors. A book that was readily available should disaster happen. It would help bring science back as part of our culture and be an inheritance.

Whatever else may be wrong with science, it still provides the best explanation we have of the material world.

It is no use even thinking of presenting such a book using magnetic or optical media, or indeed any kind of medium that needs a computer and electricity to read it. Words stored in such a form are as fleeting as the chatter of the internet and would never survive a catastrophe. Not only is the storage media itself short-lived but its reading depends upon specific hardware and software. In this technology, rapid obsolescence is usual. Modern media is less reliable for long-term storage than is the spoken word. It needs the support of a high technology that we cannot take for granted. What we need is a book written on durable paper with long-lasting print. It must be clear, unbiased, accurate and up to date ….

A book of knowledge written with authority and as splendid a read as Tyndale's Bible might need no guardians. It would earn the respect needed to place it in every home, school, library and place of worship. It would then be to hand whatever happened (*The Revenge of Gaia.*)

Information on the Archiv Lunar Library™ _from www.archivmission.org.

All other sources are cited directly in text.

3. ℼ *Lentil*
Details on the 6 bardos: "Bardo," *Wikipedia.*

Text messages with permission of N. Quastel.

Dal recipe: in *The Art of Indian Vegetarian Cooking.* Yamuna Devi, 1995. Image: K. Trainor.

4. ℼ *Snowdrop (Galanthus nivalis)*
Snowdrop descriptions are quoted from the *Wikipedia* entry for "Galanthus." The floral formula is a compact way of representing a flower's structure.

The quotation, "Its root is black…" is from Robert Fagle's 1996 translation of Book X of *The Odyssey*; the quotation beginning, "like vigilance, alertness …" is from Iain McGilchrist, *The Master and His Emissary*.

Redacted Gmail with permission of A. Huestis.

Snowdrop image: accession #V225588, UBC Herbarium, accessed through the Consortium of Pacific Northwest Herbaria:
> Canada, British Columbia: Vancouver, University Endowment Lands, Spanish Banks, at beginning of Admiralty Trail. 49.3°, -123.2°. Datum: Unknown. Georeferenced by David Rowswell. Coordinate Source: Verbatim from Collector/Sheet. In grassy area. Solitary plant. UBC: V225588 Gerald B. Straley 4044 Feb 28, 1987. Courtesy of the UBC Herbarium.

5. ▥ ◉ (*tiny house, caracol*)
Details on the Tiny House Warriors and quotations in italics from Kanahus Manuel are drawn from www.tinyhousewarriors.com.

Details on the Zapatista *caracoles* from Kurt Hackbarth and Colin Mooers, "The Zapatista Revolution Is Not Over," *The Nation*, 9 September 2019 and Leonidas Oikonomakis, "Zapatistas announce major expansion of autonomous territories," *Roar Magazine*, 19 August 2019.

Quotations in italics from Rebecca Solnit, "Revolution of the Snails: Encounters with the Zapatistas," *Common Dreams*, 16 January 2008.

6. [1] *Yellow glacier lily* (*Erythronium grandiflorum*)
Italicized descriptions of the glacier lily are drawn from *Alpine Plants of the Northwest: Wyoming to Alaska*, 2013.

Skʼémǝth. Sxwixw. Hwikwi. Máxa: words for *Erythronium grandiflorum* in Upriver Halkomelem, Secwépemc, Sahaptin, and Ktunaxa; from "Appendix 2B. Names of Native Plant Species in Indigenous Languages of Northwestern North America" in Nancy Turner's *Ancient Pathways, Ancestral Knowledge. Ethnobotany and Ecological Wisdom of Indigenous Peoples of Northwestern North America* (2014).

"Young Fruit" is a photograph of *Erythronium grandiflorum* taken at Leavenworth Ski Hill, Chelan County Washington, 47º 36' 57.08" N, 120º 39' 54.12" W. by Thayne Tuason. Creative commons, *Wikimedia*.

7. ⅠⅠ *Tardigrade*
Screenshot of "Ancient, near-indestructible 'water bears' have crash landed on the moon." CBC Radio. Posted Aug 07, 2019. Screenshot by K. Trainor.

Drawing by Finn Donegan.

Word for *seed* in various languages courtesy Google Translate and FirstVoices website.

Haiku for the Beresheet lander generated by www.languageisavirus.com/interactive-haiku-generator.php.

Imagine walking through a park: from "I plant memories in seeds: One minute interview with Karin Ljubic Fister" by Sean O'Neill, *New Scientist*, 1/16/2016. Vol. 229 Issue 3056. p.27.

8. ⅠⅠⅠ *Elysia chlorotica (chloroplast, endosymbiont)*
Image of *Volvox*, a genus of multicellular green algae, courtesy of Frank Fox (http://www.mikro-foto.de). Green algal chloroplasts contain pigments chlorophyll *a* and chlorophyll *b*. *Wikimedia*.

9. ⅠⅠⅠⅠ *The Beautiful Cell (I-glass)*
Quotations in italics from José Ortega Y. Gasset, "An essay in esthetics by way of a preface," 191.

10. ⅠⅠⅠⅠⅠ *Siit, tuuxupt, Sitka spruce (Picea sitchensis)*
Image of the Sitka spruce chloroplast genome sequence is by Lauren

Coombe et al., "Assembly of the Complete Sitka Spruce Chloroplast Genome Using 10X Genomics' GemCode Sequencing Data." *PloS ONE*, September 15, 2016.

11. † *Pacific salmon (Oncorhynchus)*

The epigraph is from a CBC report, published 25 June 2019 (https://www.cbc.ca/radio/whatonearth/how-climate-change-is-leading-to-a-redistribution-of-life-on-earth-1.5661871).

Words for chum, chinook, pink, coho, and sockeye in Russian, Korean, Japanese, and English in the collage are drawn from the North Pacific Anadromous Fish Commission (https://npafc.org/species/); Central Salish names for different varieties of Pacific salmon, are recorded in a paper by Ethan Pincott, SFU: "Contact and change in Central Salish words for salmon" (https://lingpapers.sites.olt.ubc.ca/files/2018/07/10_Central-Salish-words-for-salmon.pdf) originally published in *Papers for the International Conference on Salish and Neighbouring Languages* 53, University of British Columbia Working Papers in Linguistics 47, Marianne Huijsmans, Roger Lo, Daniel Reisinger, and Oksana Tkachman (eds.), 2018.

The story on the salmon/cedar tree cycle is recounted in "Salmon Trees" by Nancy Baron, originally published in *Equinox,* Issue 110, April/May 2000. Reprinted in *Hakai Magazine* (https://www.hakaimagazine.com/features/salmon-trees/) 22 April 2015.

My thanks to Fujan, Kent, Judy, Brian, Jacob, A., N., S., Y. for sharing their salmon dialogue.

12. ‡ *Raven (Corvus corax)*

The raven sonogram was recorded from a canoe by "Sunny" in Widgeon Creek, BC on 24 June 2019 (https://www.xeno-canto.org/484153). Screenshot: K. Trainor

The quote in italics, "A kind of knocking call…" is from "Learning to Speak Raven" *The Urban Nature Enthusiast*, 29 March 2018 (https://urbannature.blog/2018/03/29/learning-to-speak-raven/).

"The whole world was burning:" Willy Gladstone, on Raven's dream, as told to Franz Boas, *Bella Bella Texts*, reprinted (http://www.native-languages.org/heiltsukstory.htm).

13. # *Silene stenophylla (Svalbard Seed Vault)*
"75% of seed variations held by poor women farmers" is cited in "Small farmers hold the key to seed diversity: researchers," by Chris Arsenault, Thomson Reuters Foundation, 16 February 2015.

"Why can't we put all the data…" (http://www.storing-data-into-living-plant.net/experiment) by Karin Ljubič Fister and Iztok Fister Jr.

The list of types of seeds held in the Svalbard Seed Vault are taken from the Svalbard portal, an online catalogue of their seeds, using the "common name" column; other details on specific seed deposits drawn from *Seeds on Ice* by Cary Fowler, 2016.

14. # ⊗ *(Getting deeper)*
Books referenced: *A Blueprint for Survival*: *The Ecologist*, Edward Goldsmith and Robert Allen, 1972; *Our Common Future/The Brundtland Report World Commission on Environment and Development*, 1987; *Marx's Ecology: Materialism and Nature,* John Bellamy Foster, 2000; *Desert,* Anon.; *Dark Mountain Treatise*, Paul Kingsnorth and Dougald Hine; *Climate Leviathan: A Political Theory of Our Planetary Future*, Geoff Mann and Joel Wainwright, 2018.

Original demands from Extinction Rebellion, "Extinction Rebellion," *Wikipedia*.

Texts and Gmail, "getting deeper," reprinted with permission of N. Quastel.

15. ⦀ *Hymenoptera* (*honeybee, bumblebee, Vespa orientalis*)
"On Keats Island..." from "An Ethnography of Recent Muse Naming Patterns," courtesy of Jennifer Zilm.

16. + *Pacific tree frog* (*Hyla regilla, Pseudacris regilla*)
Details on *P. regilla* are drawn from the following sources:

Michael F. Benard "Natural History of the Pacific Chorus Frog *Pseudacris regilla*" (http://www.mister-toad.com/PacificTreeFrog.html)

Catherine Huybrechts, "The Biogeography of Pacific Tree Frog (*Hyla regilla*)," Geography 316, Biogeography, (http://online.sfsu.edu/bholzman/courses/Fall01%20projects/regilla.htm.htm)

Sarika Khanwilka. "'Eye' Wonder: 10 Things You Didn't Know About Frog Eyes" (https://jhwildlifefilm.wordpress.com/2014/07/28/eye-wonder-10-things-you-didnt-know-about-frog-eyes/)

Danielle V. Nelson et al. "Calling at the highway: The spatiotemporal constraint of road noise on Pacific chorus frog communication," *Ecology and Evolution*, vol. 7, 2017, pp.429-440

Sacha M. O'Regan, Wendy J. Palen, and Sean C. Anderson, "Climate warming mediates negative impacts of rapid pond drying for three amphibian species," *Ecology*, vol. 95. issue 4, 2014, pp.845-855

Claire Peasley, "The Call of the Pacific Chorus Frog: Staking out territory with sound," *Bay Nature*, Jan-March 2017

Jarad Petroske, "Rare Blue Frog Struts its Stuff at NHM," *Humboldt State Now*, 6 June 2008, (http://now.humboldt.edu/news/rare-blue-frog-struts-its-stuff-at-nhm/)

Gary J. Rose and Eliot A. Brenowitz, "Pacific treefrogs use temporal integration to differentiate advertisement from encounter calls," *Animal Behaviour*, 2002, vol. 63, pp.1183-1190

Kelly Smalling et al., "Accumulation of pesticides in Pacific chorus frogs (*Pseudacris regilla*) from California's Sierra Nevada Mountains, USA," *Environmental Toxicology & Chemistry*, Sept 2013 vol. 32 issue 9, 2026-2034

James C. Stegen, C.M. Glenger, and Lixing Sun, "The control of color change in the Pacific tree frog, *Hyla regilla*," *Canadian Journal of Zoology*, vol. 82, 2004, pp. 889-896

Wendy H. Wente and John B. Phillips, "Fixed Green and Brown Color Morphs and a Novel Color-Changing Morph of the Pacific Tree Frog *Hyla regilla*," *The American Naturalist*, vol. 162, issue 4, Oct 2003.

Photograph permissions:

12. Blue frog image, courtesy of Humboldt State University.

19. Oscillogram of tree frog chorus: Figure 1., "Pacific treefrogs use temporal integration to differentiate advertisement from encounter calls." Gary J. Rose and Eliot A. Brenowitz, *Animal Behaviour*, 2002, vol. 63, 1183-1190.

46. Photograph of egg mass, early Gosner stage, by Mark Leppin (https://www.flickr.com/people/mark_leppin/).

51. Pacific tree frog tadpole, courtesy of the Saltspring Conservancy. Photo by Purnima Govindarajulu.

58. "A Pacific Tree Frog (*Pseudacris regilla*)." Photo taken at 49° 03' 31.62" N, 122° 38' 55.69" W (California) on 8 April 2012. The High Fin Sperm Whale. (Creative Commons).

17. ⚬ SARS-CoV2

Details on SARS-CoV-2 drawn from the following sources:

"Severe acute respiratory syndrome coronavirus 2," *Wikipedia,* retrieved 5 July 2020 (https://en.wikipedia.org/wiki/Severe_acute_respiratory_syndrome_coronavirus_2)

Luis P. Villarreal, "Are Viruses Alive?" *Scientific American,* 8 August 2008 (https://www.scientificamerican.com/article/are-viruses-alive-2004/)

Nigel Brown and David Bhella, "Are Viruses Alive?" *Microbiology Society,* 10 May 2016 (https://microbiologysociety.org/publication/past-issues/what-is-life/article/are-viruses-alive-what-is-life.html).

18. ⚬ ᚁᚂᚃ ogam (*The Tree Alphabet*)

Image of the *ogam airenach*, scan of the *Auraicept na n-Éces*, ("the scholars' [*éices*] primer [*airaiccecht*]): *Book of Ballymote*, c.1390 (https://en.wikipedia.org/wiki/File:Ogham_airenach.png). Epigraph: translation from the *Auraicept na nÉces*, The Poet's Primer, by Damian McManus in *A Guide to Ogam*, 1991. McManus observes,

The letters [of ogham] are termed *feda* (pl. of *fid* 'wood, tree'), a term which can also be used specifically of the vowels, in which case the consonants may be called *táebomnai (táeb* 'side' *omnae* 'bole of a tree'), a term based apparently on the orientation of consonant symbols relative to the stemline. The latter is known in Irish as the *druim* 'ridge, edge, back' and a single score of a letter is termed *flesc* 'twig.'

He also records this story of its origins:

Ogam is from Ogma according to sound and from *og-úaim* ('perfect sewing', or 'alliteration'…) according to matter. The father of Ogam is Ogma and his hand or knife is its mother. And the first thing ever written in Ogam was [a message containing] seven *b*s in a single switch of birch sent as a warning to Lug mac Ethlenn: 'your wife will be carried away from you seven times to the *síd* ('otherworld') unless the birch protect her.' And this is why *Beithe* ('birch') is the first letter in the alphabet, because it was first written on birch.

19. ⸺ *Gaia (biosphere, carnal field)* 🌎
Blue marble image, 1972, *Earth from Apollo 17*. NASA Image #AS17-148-22727, taken by Apollo 17 astronauts. Public domain.

Epigraph from David Abram, *The Spell of the Sensuous*.

Italicized lines: Merleau-Ponty, *The Visible and the Invisible*, cited in Abram, and "Essential Elements of Tree Health" by Dr. Kim D. Coder (https://www.urban-forestry.com/assets/documents/Coder_Tree%20 Elements%20Pub%20I.pdf)

20. ⸺ T, *k'i, Betula*
Details on Ogam, the "tree language:" Damian McManus's *A Guide to Ogam.* (Maynooth, 1991.)

Gandhāran scrolls (https://www.bl.uk/collection-items/gandharan-scrolls) + *Wikipedia* entry on Kharoṣṭhī scrolls; British Library archival description;

translation of verse from Rhinoceros Sutra is my own based on a literal translation.

Bakhshali MS (https://www.wikiwand.com/en/Bakhshali_manuscript).

Bower MS: original recipe for Soma + biochemical translation: "Soma, food of the immortals according to the Bower Manuscript (Kashmir, 6th century A.D.)." Marco Leonti and Laura Casu, *Journal of Ethnopharmacology*, vol. 155, issue 1, 8 August 2014, pp.373-386.

Wiigwaasabak(https://www.cbc.ca/news/canada/sacred-ojibwa-scrolls-found-after-70-years-1.227492).

Gulag postcard on birchbark (http://www.gulagmuseum.org/showObject.do?object=38988890&language=2), postcard inventory TR424; translation into English by Google translate; *Gulag Letters* by Arsenii Formakov.

Gramoty fragments, "Onfim wuz here..." by Justin E. H. Smith; http://gramoty.ru/birchbark/document/show/novgorod/521/ and fragments 837, 521, 199; https://en.wikipedia.org/wiki/Onfim.

Recipe for Birch Wine: John Worlidge's 1676 *Vinetum Britannicum: Or a Treatise of Cider and Other Wines and Drinks*.

Details on birch baskets in the pre-Kamloops period (roughly 2000 years before present time) are found in "Barking up the right tree: understanding birch bark artifacts from the Canadian Plateau, British Columbia" by Shannon Croft and Rolf W. Mathewes. In *BC Studies*, vol. 180, pp.83-122.

Betula papyrifera: Much of the technical descriptions of birch throughout has been drawn from a monograph on *Betula papyrifera* Marsh by the US Federal Forest Service.

Words for paper birch in First Nation languages: firstvoices.com (https://www.firstvoices.com/explore/FV/sections/Data/search/birch) and

"Appendix 2B. Names of Native Plant Species in Indigenous Languages of Northwestern North America," supplemental to Nancy J. Turner's *Ancient Pathways, Ancestral Knowledge. Ethnobotany and Ecological Wisdom of Indigenous Peoples of Northwestern North America,* McGill-Queen's University Press, 2014 (https://dspace.library.uvic.ca/bitstream/handle/1828/5091/ Appendix%202B%20%20UVicSpace%20Indigenous%20names%20 of%20native%20species_BIG.pdf?sequence=5&isAllowed=y).

Acknowledgements

I gratefully acknowledge the assistance of a 2020 Canada Council for the Arts grant and a 2020 British Columbia Arts Council grant.

Heartfelt gratitude to:

Michael Mirolla of Guernica Editions.
Editor Anna van Valkenburg for her thoughtful suggestions and beautiful attention to detail.
Typesetter Jill Ronsley for heroic work on a complex layout.
Errol F. Richardson for the cover design, which incorporates a blueprint of the Svalbard Seedbank.

And to the editors who first published many of these poems:

I. Wildfire
CV2: "Wallflower," "Boreal," and "The Beautiful Cell."
The Antigonish Review: "Little Mountain."
The Fiddlehead: "Paper Birch."
The Malahat Review: "Manna."
Arc: "Wildfire" and "North Road."
The Antigonish Review: "Little Mountain," "Ora."
Otoliths (Australia): "T, *k'i*, betula," "Tardigrade," "Blackmud."
Dalhousie Review: "Whitemud."
"Wildfire" and "Little Mountain" were anthologized in *Fire Season I* (2020); "Seed 1, Shelter," "Paper birch," and "North Road" were anthologized in *Fire Season II* (2022). Both volumes edited by Liz Toohey-Wiese and Amory Abbott.
Ecological Citizen: "Say Nuth Khaw Yum."

II. Seeds

Dark Matter: Women Witnessing (US): "Shelter." Nominated for a 2021 Pushcart Prize.

ISLE: International Studies in Literature and Environment (US): "Snowdrop (*Galanthus nivalis*)."

Anthropocenes: Human, Inhuman, Posthuman (UK): "Poet's Statement + Excerpt from 'Seeds': 'Yellow glacier lily (*Erythronium grandiflorum,*)' '*Siit, tuuxupt*, Sitka spruce,' and '*Hymenoptera* (honeybee, bumblebee, *Vespa orientalis*).'"

Cold Mountain Review (US): "Tonquin" and "Pacific Tree Frog."

Ecocene: Cappadocia Journal of Environmental Humanities (Turkey): "Snail, tiny house, *caracol*" and "SARS-Cov-2."

Deep Wild (US): "Desolation: 2 drafts" (1st draft only).

The Journal of Wild Culture (US): "Seed 12, Common raven," "Seed 13, 'Silene stenophylla,'" "Seed 14, XR / Getting deeper."

Ecozon@ (Spain): "Seed 8, *Elysia chlorotica*," "Seed 19, Gaia."

Dark Mountain (UK): "Seed 11, Pacific salmon."

"Seed 18, Ogam, the tree alphabet" was anthologized in *Worth More Standing*, edited by Christine Lowther.

"Paper Birch" won *The Fiddlehead*'s 2019 Gustafson Prize.

"Ora" won the 2018 Great Blue Heron Contest (*The Antigonish Review*). My thanks to the judges for these contests.

My thanks also to Art Song 2020 for facilitating collaborative work with composer Yi-Ning Li on "Blackmud" and to Yi-Ning for her generous musical interpretation of the poem.

Hazel Fairbairn has been a stalwart, brilliant collaborator, creating sound-scapes for the poetry films I've made from "Seeds." "SARS-CoV-2" screened at Seattle's 2022 Cadence Video Poetry Festival, as part of its "As the wind is breathing" showcase. "Tardigrade" appeared at Copenhagen's Det Poetiske Fonotek's Nature and Culture International Poetry Film Festival 2021 and the Drumshanbo Written Word Poetry Film Festival

2023. "Lentil" appeared at the Bloomsday Literary Festival 2023 and the Midwest Video Poetry Fest 2023.

N. + A. for allowing me to incorporate their words, texts + Gmail into these poems.

Jennifer Zilm, for allowing me to quote a line from "An Ethnography of Recent Muse Naming Patterns" in *Hymenoptera*, and for scrutinizing *A blueprint for survival* one desultory May day in 2023 at San Marcos La Laguna, Guatemala, to the sound of distant roosters.

These poems were written primarily on the unceded, traditional homelands of the xʷməθkʷəyəm, Skwxwú7mesh, Tsleil-Waututh, Qiqéyt, kʷikʷəƛ̓əm, and Snuneymuxw First Nations. A few were written in Edmonton on Treaty 6 territory.

"The Beautiful Cell" was written on a ferry crossing the Salish Sea.

About the Author

KIM TRAINOR is the granddaughter of an Irish banjo player and a Polish faller who worked in logging camps around Port Alberni in the 1930s. Her earlier books are *Karyotype* (Brick Books, 2015), *Ledi* (Book*hug, 2018), shortlisted for the Raymond Souster award, and *A thin fire runs through me* (icehouse poetry / Goose Lane Editions, 2023). Her poems have appeared in *Anthropocenes (AHIP), Ecocene, ISLE, Ecozon@, Dark Mountain* (UK) and *Fire Season I and II* (Vancouver). Her poetry films have screened at Zebra Poetry Film Festival (Berlin) and at +the Institute [for experimental art] (Athens), as well as in Dublin and Seattle. Her current project is "walk quietly / ts'ekw'unshun kws qututhun," a guided walk at Hwlhits'um (Canoe Pass) in Delta, BC, in collaboration with Amy-Claire Huestis featuring contributions from artists, scientists, and Hwlitsum and Cowichan knowledge holders.

Printed by Imprimerie Gauvin
Gatineau, Québec